Fostering Connection

Building
Social and Emotional Health
in Children and Teens

Dr. Tish Taylor

Fostering Connection: Building Social and Emotional Health in Children and Teens
by Dr. Tish Taylor

Copyright © 2022

All rights reserved. No part of this book may be reproduced in any form without permission in writing from the author. Reviewers may quote brief passages in reviews.

Medical Disclaimer

This information is not intended as a substitute for the advice provided by your physician or other healthcare professional. Do not use the information in this book for diagnosing or treating a health problem or disease, or prescribing medication or other treatment.

Artwork: Courtney Foat
Editor: Jenny Bartoy
Publishing and Design Services: MelindaMartin.me

ISBN: 978-0-9842725-1-8 (paperback), 978-0-9842725-2-5 (epub)

Contents

Introduction 1

Chapter 1 Who is Showing Up? 3

Chapter 2 How Do I Want to Show Up? 13

Chapter 3 Connectors and Disconnectors 19

Chapter 4 Meet the Connectors 25

Chapter 5 Meet the Disconnectors 61

Chapter 6 Building and Strengthening Connector Skills 91

References 106

About the Author 107

INTRODUCTION

Fostering Connection was written for counselors and parents who are looking for resources to help them build social and emotional health in children and teens. To help reach this goal, I developed the Who Is Showing Up? System for use in my child psychology practice, and I will be sharing it with you in this book. Who Is Showing Up? presents an easy-to-understand system of concepts, characters, and images to assist children, teens, parents, and other adults in addressing difficult behaviors. It teaches self-awareness around non-compliant, argumentative, and inflexible behaviors, explains the counterparts to those behaviors through characters, images, and concepts, and outlines adaptive and coping responses. This system is ideal for individuals with Oppositional Defiant Disorder (ODD) or Attention-Deficit Hyperactivity Disorder (ADHD), or those of a strong-willed nature who tend to be non-compliant, argumentative, and inflexible in their thinking.

The Who is Showing Up? System offers an innovative approach meant to build and improve relationships within families and between individuals. It is helpful for parents, children, teens, educators, and mental health clinicians. The goal is to better communicate difficulties between adults and teens as well as to increase self-understanding.

My hope is to help you build and maintain a positive connection with your child, within your family, with your student, and within your relationships. In my practice as a psychologist, I find that equipping patients with tools, common language, and simple strategies tends to lead to effective results. For the Who Is Showing Up? System, I have conceptualized characters that illustrate a mindset, a mood, or a pattern of behavior. This can help you determine what character is showing up in your interactions and how this character may impact the situation.

Identifying "who is showing up" in another person or child is often easier, but recognizing how *you* show up or respond is also important. When specific characters show up regularly in a relationship, a pattern has been developed and likely established. Humans build from these patterns. In close relationships, patterns lead to a quick reactionary cycle or protective mode that can reinforce a cycle of negative interactions. My goal is to help you quickly identify what is happening, label it, investigate it, and choose a wise response. This system is meant to decrease negative interaction patterns within your important relationships. The Who Is Showing Up? System will bring you more insight and an ability to respond effectively when communicating with your child, student, or client.

CHAPTER 1

WHO IS SHOWING UP?

How Do I Show Up?

Let's start with a self-reflection exercise:

Imagine that you are watching a video of yourself interacting with your child or the child with whom you are in frequent contact. Consider a typical challenging scenario, or one that causes you frustration. What do you see? What does your tone of voice sound like? What do your facial expressions convey? What does the child experience? Take the time to honestly self-reflect.

This exercise can help you assess how you show up. An objective perspective can be challenging to achieve because we typically think about how the other person is showing up, and you may be more attuned to them rather than yourself. However, for this exercise, consider the standpoint of an outsider observer: what would they see in you? And is this what you want them to experience?

How Does the Interaction Begin?

Psychological researcher John Gottman's work (1999) is specific to marriages and committed adult relationships, but his work offers important takeaways in regard to how a person shows up in a situation, including how they initially communicate (Claire & Werner-Wilson, 2013). Gottman emphasizes the "start-up" or how one enters a situation: whether that start-up is positive or negative can have a tremendous impact on the outcome of the interaction. He found that 96% of the time the outcome of a 15-minute conversation can be predicted within the first three minutes. When negative communication techniques are used—such as criticism, complaining, sarcasm, insults, name-calling, ignoring, or withdrawing—negative responses and interactions will ensue.

Assuming that all close relationships bear similarities, it is reasonable to expect that how we show up with children will follow the same principles. If we show up irritated, critical, or sarcastic, in response a child or teen will likely become defensive, lash out, or emotionally protect themselves in some way. They will not be primed to enter the situation in a vulnerable, communicative, or self-reflective way. To improve chances of a positive outcome, communication should begin with a thoughtful and caring approach.

Example:

Parent: "Why haven't you cleaned your room? I have told you three times now! What is wrong with you?"

Child: "I'm getting to it. Stop yelling at me!"

Parent: "I am tired of you not listening to me. Just do it and do it now!"

Child: "Leave me alone!"

This scenario could go on with an escalating exchange or end with the adult leaving. Either way, the outcome is negative and it is difficult to determine if the room will get cleaned or not. If feelings between parent and child remain unpleasant and this type of interaction becomes a pattern, the relationship will grow more strained, compliance will be less likely in the future, and instances of negative interactions and feelings will increase.

Am I Promoting a Quality Relationship?

Research has shown that the emotional synchronicity or connectedness between a parent and child as well as the perceived quality of the parent-child relationship have an impact on a child's behavioral patterns (Booker et al, 2016; Miller-Slough et al, 2016). When a parent and their child are aligned in how they respectively understand an issue, in how much they understand and communicate their present emotion, and in how focused they are on the same subject, their ability to work together toward a mutual goal will improve. Emotional warmth, connection, and decreased conflict improve the perception and quality of the relationship, thus promoting a decrease in negative behaviors from children.

For example, one may improve the quality of their relationship with a child by using a tone that reflects connection versus adopting a "do it now" or "listen to me this instant" attitude. Even if a child has been frustrating or noncompliant, consider whether a harsh or hurried approach will work in the long term. In a specific instance it may, but if this type of interaction becomes a pattern, it will become more ineffectual than helpful. Why? Because individuals tend not to comply with a "do as I say, now" type of expectation for long, since it negates connection and demands a one-way type of relationship. Of course, situations related to safety, where someone could be harmed physically or emotionally, and situations that carry a high negative consequence quotient may require a direct approach. However, most instances do not.

Disconnecting Variations in Adults

Adults display disconnection through various communication patterns or styles. Noticing your style or interaction patterns can allow for increased awareness, particularly in terms of how communication is received by your child. Of course, no one sticks to one style all of the time, but tendencies can be identified. In addition, this self-awareness can assist you in determining how you want to be received and what you really want to convey. Examples of communication styles are listed next.

Disconnecting Variations in Adults		
Style	Physical Communication	Verbal Communication
Stressed and Frenzied	This typically includes a stressed and frenzied facial expression and tone.	"Hurry, hurry, hurry!" "This has got to get done now!" "We are out of time. You have to move!"
Irritated	This typically includes an irritated facial expression and tone.	"Aren't you done yet? Come on!" "I'm still waiting…"
Demanding	This typically includes a disapproving facial expression and tone.	"I said now, and no more excuses!" "I expect more from you."
Accusatory	This typically includes an irritated and disapproving facial expression and tone.	"I knew that you would screw this up." "You are the one who keeps messing up around here."
Yelling or Angry	This typically includes an angry and disapproving facial expression and very loud tone.	Any of the above with a greater degree of anger or disgust, along with yelling or screaming.

Many instances of a child's behavior can indeed create frustration, stress, and anger. The question is: what outcome do you want? And how do you want to communicate that? To teach a child to manage their emotions and their behavior, we must model this for them.

Being the Adult in a Difficult Situation without Disconnecting

In any given situation with your child, thinking about your goal is a key step. The goal could be obtaining compliance in the moment, getting to school on time, having your child follow through with simple tasks (even though they have been asked multiple times), or just trying to have a civil conversation without getting attitude. But above all these, I would contend that your goal is to lead by example. Respond with your goal in mind, not allowing your stressed or frustrated emotions to lead the way.

A child will tend to follow your example—although they may hold it against you if they are angry. Consider your goal, be it to gain compliance while maintaining a dignified exchange, to arrive to an appointment on time while remaining composed, or maybe just to get to school while avoiding a huge argument. Each scenario can go in many directions so you must focus on the wanted behavior as well as the avenue you will use to get there.

Goals should include the behaviors that you want to see or to increase in your child. Venting frustrations will not lead you to this goal; instead it will sidetrack you. When removed from the situation, evaluate whether the problem is a recurring one and begin to apply problem-solving to the specific issue. For example, if a child is frequently late and doesn't seem to grasp or monitor time, how can you set up a system or plan to improve this? If a child tends to be snarky or respond in a disrespectful tone, how can you bring this to light and work together with more connectedness to improve respectful interactions?

While I will not go into detail about the biological or environmental influences that may fuel adult reactions, it is an important area of self-reflection. If you notice a pattern of negative or frustrated responses, I encourage you to work to recognize its source. Consider whether biological reasons, patterns from your own childhood, or current stressors may be at play—any or all can influence how you show up.

Notice How Your Child Is Showing Up

Do I Stop to Notice How the Other Person Is Responding?

What nonverbal and verbal signs is your child giving? It is important to recognize if the child has stopped responding in a positive way, if they are overwhelmed, or if the entire process of communication is ineffective. If one or all of these occur, the interaction—and consequently, feelings and behavior too—will become more negative. Stop and assess whether your communication barrages the child. Does it quickly lead to an overwhelmed, shut-down, defensive, or combative stance? If so, communication and interactions are rendered ineffectual. Stepping outside of your own thoughts and convictions and noticing your child's response to communication can assist you in navigating the situation more effectively.

Navigating a child's negative response is different than giving clear and specific directions. I do not want to confuse the two. There are certainly times when directions or expectations need to be stated clearly and simply. However, it is often what comes after these statements that determines whether interactions are effectual or not. If the child openly accepts directions and expectations and then complies, additional communication is typically not required. But when the child does not comply, the situation calls for more observation into the line of interaction. My goal is to help you work toward connection and away from disconnection in these instances.

Disconnecting Variations in Children

Just like adults, children and teens can display a variety of communication styles or patterns. Noticing how a child shows up can assist you in labeling their behavior and communicating in a manner that allows for recognition and understanding. In turn, this can lead to modeling another way to communicate.

Disconnecting Variations in Children		
Style	Physical Communication	Verbal Communication
Irritated or Irritable	This typically includes an angry or irritated tone.	"What do you want?!" "Leave me alone!"
Defensive	This includes any response that rejects blame or responsibility.	"I didn't do it!" "It's not my fault!"
Avoiding	This includes avoiding, ignoring, shifting the topic, or reacting in a highly emotional way.	"I don't know what you're talking about." "Okay, fine. Whatever."
Blaming	This includes the child shirking their responsibility in the situation and pointing the finger at someone else.	"It's your fault that this happened." "But she did this to me!" "I didn't do anything; you did!"
Dismissive	"Whatever." "Okay, sure."	This includes eye rolls, indications of not caring, and statements conveying the issue is inconsequential.

Observe the Specific Interaction

Let's return to self-reflection. Notice how your personal way of showing up in a situation may prompt the child's reaction. Did the beginning of the interaction trigger a disconnection? It is important to notice where this disconnection began in order to address improvement. The child may instead be reacting to a long pattern of disconnecting start-ups. In other words, the child may be primed to react due to expected and practiced interaction patterns. If so, it will take more time and effort to undo a disconnecting response. If, however, the adult interactions are typically connecting, it can be important to identify anything internal to the child that could be prompting the response.

Because interactions are bi-directional, the way a child shows up can then influence how the interaction continues. If a child shows up in a disconnecting manner, emotions are likely to be sparked and a negative interaction may then begin, as adults can also become accustomed to a child's patterns. Sometimes, where one ends and the other begins can be difficult to determine. Therefore, being able to observe, label, and recognize a path for interactions is a big step in maintaining a more positive connection.

Childhood Disorders that Influence Disconnection

Some disorders in children can increase the likelihood of disconnecting behaviors. Due to the nature of the disorder, parents often notice behavioral patterns that tend toward disconnecting communication. Within my professional experience, I have witnessed the following disorders influencing disconnection (American Psychiatric Association, 2013):

- *Oppositional Defiant Disorder (ODD)* is a disorder characterized by patterns of angry and irritable moods, argumentative behavior, and noncompliant or defiant behavior. It may also include vindictive behavior, anger outbursts, blaming others for behaviors or mistakes, and purposely annoying others. These behavioral patterns occur to a more significant degree and with more persistence than in most children their age. ODD frequently occurs in combination with ADHD, Autism Spectrum Disorders (ASDs), and/or mood disorders. Strained family dynamics and parent-child relationships can also increase the chances of a child exhibiting this type of profile.

- *Attention-Deficit Hyperactivity Disorder (ADHD)* is a disorder characterized by either an inattentive presentation, a hyperactive-impulsive presentation, or a combined presentation. Children with this disorder show persistent difficulties with task management, organization, and sustained attention and typically demonstrate distractibility, hyperactivity, and/or impulsivity. Depending on the disorder's specific type, the child may exhibit a combination of some or most of these factors. If the severity is greater, the disability and disruption to daily life are more pronounced. This often includes difficulties with transitions, including mental transitions or cognitive shifts, time management skills, prioritization skills, motivational challenges, and task completion issues.

- *Mood Disorders* can vary between major depressive disorders, dysthymia (persistent lower mood), bipolar disorder, or disruptive mood dysregulation (which is characterized by a persistently irritable mood and frequent quick and angry outbursts). Mood disorders often prompt a child to exhibit more irritability and anger, stressed or overwhelmed behavior, and decreased coping with everyday stressors.

- *Anxiety Disorders* are relatively varied and, depending on their type and severity, can present as stress and fear, but also as irritability and resistance. Anxiety disorders that show stronger resistant patterns and disengagement include intense phobias, Obsessive Compulsive Disorder, separation anxiety, social anxiety, and persistent generalized anxiety disorder.

These psychiatric disorders can impact various aspects of a child's functioning including how a child might show up under certain circumstance or at certain times. It is important to note that while various children can be diagnosed with the same disorder, how it presents is unique to them.

CHAPTER 2

How Do I Want to Show Up?

Values

In the process of truly knowing how you want to show up with your child or those you serve, an important first step is to establish your values—be they individual, familial, and/or professional. Going through the exercise of clearly establishing those values within your own mind makes the communication of behaviors and expectations much easier. It also makes the introduction of the characters within this book more applicable and simpler to communicate.

I urge you to go through the exercise of solidifying your values for yourself and your family. Identify what values drive your decisions, your reactions, and the rules you put in place for children. A helpful resource for this process can be found at https://www.actmindfully.com.au/wp-content/uploads/2019/07/Values_Checklist_-_Russ_Harris.pdf. The list provided in this document, as well as the accompanying exercise, can help clarify what values are meaningful for you, as well as for your family and children. This in turn will assist you in recognizing when you behave in a manner aligned with your values—or not. Remember that children encode and model what they observe more than what they are told.

Examples of common values include:

- *Honesty*: be honest and sincere with others and self.
- *Respect*: show positive regard to others and self.
- *Respect of property*: value one's own property as well as others' property.
- *Education and knowledge*: seek and value learning, education, and knowledge.

- *Work ethic*: believe in honest and hard work, giving appropriate and full effort.
- *Kindness*: show kindness and consideration to others.
- *Compassion*: demonstrate kindness toward others in pain or suffering.
- *Acceptance*: be aware and open to others and self.
- *Love*: be affectionate and caring to self and others.
- *Integrity*: act consistently within one's strong values, given different situations.
- *Being loved*: value care and love from others.
- *Achievement*: hold accomplishments in high esteem.
- *Happiness*: value contentment and joy.
- *Leadership*: lead others in a positive direction.
- *Peace*: value serenity and tranquility
- *Justice*: uphold fairness for all and within groups.
- *Safety*: value feeling secure and protected.
- *Spirituality*: connect with a higher power or something bigger than self

Am I the Perfect Parent?

The short answer is "no." Many of us strive to be, but this expectation is unrealistic. More important questions are: do you convey and live your values to the best of your ability? Do you strive to show up in a supportive, nurturing, and positive manner? Are you able to adjust to each child (if you have more than one) in a way that is a good fit for them and then manage those differences with your other children? Overall, we want to show up in a manner that reflects our values and provides our children a loving and supportive environment. However, each child is different and therefore, what one child needs, another may not need in the same way. Being able to pivot and recognize what is a good fit for each child takes thought, understanding, and practice. You can improve your parenting skills, but this requires making intentional choices based on clear values, as well as practicing the manner in which these choices are delivered. You may not be the perfect parent, but you can strive to be close.

Why Am I This way?

Often the way we parent reflects our own childhood or current life situation or challenges. It is helpful to understand if you are triggered by certain behaviors. Here are some important questions to ask yourself:

- Am I reactionary? If so, what triggers or internal traits make me more reactionary?
- Do I keep my intentions and values in mind when having a difficult interaction?
- Am I fatigued? If so, what does my fatigued response look like?
- Do I lose my patience or temper? If so, how does this appear to others?
- How do I feel after more difficult interactions?
    - Do I believe my child deserved it?
    - Do I feel connected or disconnected?
    - Do I try to move on and ignore my feelings of disconnection or guilt?
    - Other thoughts?

Where Did All of This Come From?

Consider your experience with important individuals in your life, specifically your parents and family of origin. Your context for interactions begins there. What did difficult interactions look like? How did you experience them? What did you learn from them, both positive and negative? This thoughtful self-reflection can provide some insight into your behavior, especially parenting behavior. If there is a complicated or painful answer to some of these questions, it may behoove you to explore them with a trained mental health provider.

What Do I Want to Keep And What Do I Want to Change?

Considering what has been covered in this chapter so far, what parenting behaviors do you want to maintain? These should be behaviors that provide your child and your family what they need emotionally, psychologically, spiritually, and physically. Now consider what you want to change. These may be big or small changes, but ultimately making these changes is better for all involved.

Scenario: Sarah is extremely frustrated with her daughter, Chloe. Chloe is bright and likes to challenge her mother's requests, argue a point, and derail a request with counterpoints. Sarah is used to this behavior, but it drives her crazy nonetheless. She has tried to reason with Chloe and establish her authority, but Chloe's behavior continues. In certain instances, Sarah ends up screaming at Chloe and threatening to take her phone away for the rest of the school year.

If Sarah stops to check her values and think about how she wants to show up, she can approach interactions with Chloe more creatively and communicate more clearly. Sarah values kindness and calm. She wants a mutually respectful relationship with her daughter. She could calmly and plainly state that the request is not up for negotiation or debate. The direction and expectation stand: Chloe's homework must be finished before she can hang out with her friends. It is up to Chloe whether she follows through or not, but either way there are consequences to her decision. Sarah is not willing to debate the fine points of the expectation, because education is a clear value that Chloe has understood for a long time and that Sarah now reiterates.

What I Want to Maintain (It's a Keeper!)	Why This Is Valuable
1. Communicating clearly and calmly.	I can communicate my values yet not show up frustrated and mad, which derails the situation and fails to address important issues.
2. Staying focused on my values in difficult situations.	This maintains the basis for my decisions and behavior as well as consistently teaches my child those things I believe to be important.
3. Showing care, love, and concern for my daughter, even when I am frustrated with her.	This reinforces my established values and maintains a strong connection with Chloe.

What I Want to Change (You're Outta Here!)	What I Want to Replace It With
1. Yelling and screaming.	Communicating calmly and clearly, even if I have to take a short break in order to compose myself.
2. Threatening big consequences that are not followed through due to a reactionary response.	Stating reasonable and specific consequences (both positive and negative) to Chloe's choice. For example, "You can choose to finish your homework and then have about an hour with your friends, or you can choose to delay it, be upset about it, and not finish it, and miss time with your friends today."

How Do I Want to Show Up?

Now consider your own interactions with your child. What behaviors do you want to keep and what do you want to change? Complete the table below to clearly define what they are for you. It can be very helpful to do this exercise for your interactions with each individual child.

What I Want to Maintain (It's a Keeper!)	Why This Is Valuable
1.	
2.	
3.	

What I Want to Change (You're Outta Here!)	What I Want to Replace It With
1.	
2.	
3.	

CHAPTER 3

Connectors and Disconnectors

In order to clearly define and contextualize how we connect and disconnect within our interactions, I have created a set of characters that illustrate specific behaviors. These characters can assist children, teens, parents, and adults in identifying and understanding how they show up in a given situation as well as recognizing a productive way to do so. These characters are labeled Connectors and Disconnectors.

Connectors

What is a Connector?

When a Connector shows up, this character presents an understanding of self and others. Connectors are able to recognize the consequences of both disconnection and connection, and they desire to live with more connection, even when it is difficult. A Connector can stop and assess the situation, other persons, and themselves. They show some level of emotional intelligence: they can understand their own feelings, the components of the situation, and another person's emotions. In addition, they can utilize strategies to help manage their feelings, uphold their values, and maintain relationships.

Why Be a Connector?

The better question may be "why not?" Why not live a life where emotions are expressed but regulated, and where your relationships show care, love, and respect? There is much to gain from fostering positive relationships and much to lose from disconnection. Connection is easier to find in some relationships than in others—especially a strong connection. However, consider how your skill set (or lack thereof) might come into play. What if you could achieve greater connection and a more satisfying relationship with at least one person? Learning new skills seems worth it.

Why Be a Connector In the Face of Disrespectful Behavior?

This can be a tough proposition. In the face of disrespectful behavior, maintaining one's values is difficult and showing up in a manner that differs from how you are treated may go against a natural response. When you respond in kind, do you feel vindicated by your response or like you have the upper hand? Do you feel that you "showed them who is boss" or that you know more than they do? Let that sink in and consider what you or your child gains from this type of interaction. It may help to consider how you feel in the long run after these negative interactions.

As a parent, you do need to set boundaries and limits. The question is how to enforce these boundaries and limits. Do you want to do so in a way that nurtures, guides, teaches, and ultimately connects? I have yet to find a parent who does not acquiesce to this question. We all long for connection. My hope is to help you recognize when your Connectors should be showing up and practice this skill set.

Disconnectors

What is a Disconnector?

A Disconnector creates or perpetuates negativity, conflict, and disconnection within interactions. Disconnectors maintain conflict, lack of compromise or mutual understanding, and ultimately disconnection. The emotions that fuel them are negative. I'd like to note here that negative emotions are not a bad thing. But acting on them or responding to negative behavior with negativity in return can begin to color a relationship accordingly.

The more we practice something, the better we get at it. It stands to reason that the more a person engages in relationships as a Disconnector, the better they get at disconnecting. Ultimately, this pattern leads to more internal negativity and conflict within relationships. Deep down, no one really wants this in their life. The concept of the Disconnector characters represents a targeted and non-threatening approach to assist individuals in understanding how they are showing up and determining whether that is consistent with their values.

Why Do Disconnectors Show Up?

Disconnectors show up within children and teens for different reasons. This age group tends to lack skill or understanding. Some young individuals are not readily aware or tuned in to what is called *theory of mind*. Theory of mind is a mental state that allows a person to not only assess how they may think about a situation but also recognize that another person may think differently about it (Doherty, 2009). Some children may have difficulty with this because they only operate from their frame of reference. Theory of mind is a developmental skill, meaning that it improves as children age. Most typically developing children begin to understand this concept at a young age. Children with an Autism Spectrum Disorder often have a more difficult time with theory of mind. Some children with ADHD and Oppositional Defiant Disorder can also demonstrate weakness with this skill.

Disconnectors sometimes show up because children and teens can be very focused on their point of view or reference point and have a hard time considering another person's, even if they could. They are cognitive and developmentally capable of understanding that someone else may have a different perspective, but they tend to be closed-minded and believe that they themselves are correct in how they interpret the situation. Their perspective tends to be egocentric, with little consideration for another.

Defensiveness and lack of vulnerability can also cause Disconnectors to show up. Vulnerability—admitting one's own shortcomings—can be challenging. Not allowing themselves to be vulnerable or humble increases a child's sense of power or control. This sense of power may feel comfortable and help them maintain the sense that they are "right" and there is no need to change their behavior. This type of defensiveness can occur if parents often show up in a disconnecting manner.

Finally, another reason Disconnectors might show up is lack of skill. A lack of practice at connection means that disconnection is the only type of skill within one's toolbox. One primary goal of the concepts in this book is to teach more adaptive connecting skills to children and teens.

What Is the Result of Being a Disconnector?

Showing up with frequent Disconnector behavior results in our relationships and sense of closeness suffering. If disconnection occurs once in a while, along with typically connecting behaviors, that is not such a big deal. However, if Disconnectors show up more frequently or in a familiar pattern, then we feel less trust, less positive regard, and more defensiveness with the person exhibiting disconnecting behavior. Modeling and showing children and teens connecting ways to interact allows them to develop the necessary skills for more fulfilling relationships. It's best to avoid establishing a cycle of coerciveness and negative interaction, or one that gives Disconnectors more power.

Do We Ever Need the Disconnectors?

Disconnectors can come about through trauma, mistreatment, or patterns from adults that have proven to be untrustworthy. This can mean inconsistency in adult responses and interactions, including inconsistency in behaviors that have the best interest of the child at heart. Disconnectors can evolve from a defense mechanism needed to maintain emotional safety. The child does not allow themselves to trust the relationship with the adult or the adult's intentions, which causes less hurt. If the situation includes more complicated, inconsistent, or traumatic experiences, therapeutic work may be needed with the child. Helping them differentiate these behaviors will deepen their understanding and will help them know when or how they want to apply certain behaviors.

Scenarios Illustrating Connectors and Disconnectors

Scenario: Richard and Henry are playing soccer with friends in their neighborhood. Richard and Henry disagree about whether a ball was offsides and whose team should have possession of it. Richard is convinced that he is right because he has played soccer for many years and knows the rules. Henry is convinced that he is right because he also plays soccer and has watched matches on television; he insists he knows the correct rules of soccer.

Both boys become frustrated and argue with each other, although the argument has little hope of being resolved without some type of compromise. Henry becomes angrier and tells Richard that he is a "know-it-all" and a "jerk." At this point, Richard concedes by saying, "Fine, Henry. We will do it your way, just to move on." Richard doesn't like it, but he realizes that this situation is going nowhere and he doesn't want to have a big argument.

In this scenario, Richard demonstrates more connecting skills: he is able to control his emotions and avoid name-calling or escalating an argument. He is also able to realize that the situation is not worth a huge argument that would ultimately end the game or have everyone leave upset. Henry, on the other hand, shows more disconnection: he does not concede or consider a point other than his own, chooses to escalate the situation, and engages in a more intense argument to prove that he is correct.

Scenario: Jacqueline and Aisha are sisters. They bicker and argue like most siblings. However, Jacqueline, the oldest, tends to be more domineering and insistent about how things should be. Aisha becomes quickly frustrated and irritated with Jacqueline. When Jacqueline tries to tell Aisha something that she should be doing, Aisha yells at Jacqueline to "Shut up, you are not my boss!" then runs off to her room and slams the door. In these instances, Jacqueline shows disconnection in her approach with Aisha: she does not consider how she may be showing up to Aisha-bossy and insensitive. And Aisha shows disconnecting skills by becoming overwhelmed and upset; acting out of emotion; and not being able to communicate effectively.

CHAPTER 4

Meet the Connectors

The **Connectors** are a group of characters who, when experiencing emotions, show up in a way that maintains healthy relationships and interactions with others. These characters use strategies that help them manage their feelings, understand and accept these feelings, connect with others, and respond to them in a respectful way. Connectors help maintain a higher order of peace and dignity. No relationship or person is perfect, but striving for healthy, peaceful, and dignified interactions is a worthy goal for ourselves and our relationships. Each Connector will be described in detail in this chapter and they are presented in this order: Feelings Mind, Feelings Investigator, Helpful Coach, Shoes, Two-Way Street, Captain Courageous, and Mending in Action, as well as Healthy Tools.

To access a pdf version of all Connector images, go to:
www.tishtaylor.com/Connectors/pdf

Meet the Connectors

Connector	Skills
Feelings Mind	1. Label feelings. 2. Recognize body sensations. 3. Assess thoughts. 4. Acknowledge mood state. 5. Recognize mindset.
Feelings Investigator	1. Recognize one's own feelings as well as the likely feelings of others. 2. Assess the context, including what others expect and how the context may influence emotions. 3. Consider options in response. 4. Determine what would improve the situation for everyone.
Helpful Coach	1. Recognize when to call a time-out. 2. Use positive motivation. 3. Implement problem-solving. 4. Ask for help.
Shoes	1. Understand that others have their own internal experience. 2. Acknowledge that others have different life experiences. 3. Recognize that another person's experiences may cause them to react differently. 4. Seek to understand another person's experience through evidence or active listening.
Two-Way Street	1. Recognize that others have different thoughts, opinions, and perspectives. 2. Show willingness to understand another's perspective. 3. Acknowledge and respect another's perspective. 4. Accept that group perspectives exist and differ.
Captain Courageous	1. Let down defenses. 2. Practice humility. 3. Communicate effectively. 4. Maintain a caring attitude even when hurt, angered, or upset.
Mending in Action	1. Use communication that reconciles and seeks to bring peace. 2. Show compassion and respect to others. 3. Engage in repair such as apologies and a willingness to listen. 4. Commit to a different path in the future.

The Feelings Mind

The Feelings Mind is a character who demonstrates perceptive insight into their own feelings. In general, this Connector understands their emotions in a given moment or situation. The Feelings Mind grasps that these feelings will not last forever and will change over a short amount of time. The Feelings Mind displays a hierarchy of skills. These include labeling their emotions, recognizing the body sensations associated with how they feel emotionally, and differentiating feelings from thoughts.

Common Skills of the Feelings Mind

Skill 1: Label feelings.

The Feelings Mind is skilled at recognizing and labeling feelings. Below is a list of common emotions. Lists, especially with picture examples, are helpful in identifying how one may feel in a situation. Note that when frustration and anger show up, it is common for individuals not to recognize that they also feel disappointed. When a person is developing the skill of recognizing and labeling feelings, a broader list of emotions can help understand the full range of emotions, especially in more complex situations.

- Happy
- Content
- Frustrated
- Angry
- Disappointed
- Sad
- Anxious
- Fearful
- Suspicious
- Shy
- Overwhelmed
- Irritated
- Peaceful
- Confused
- Surprised
- Ashamed
- Guilty
- Worried
- Hopeful

Skill 2: Recognize body sensations.

The Feelings Mind assists a person in differentiating emotions from body sensations or physical states, then in understanding how physical states or sensations may be related to emotions. It also recognizes how emotions and body sensations may influence each other in a given situation. Again, using a list with picture cues can be helpful in developing this skill. Examples of physical sensations include:

- Tired
- Hungry
- Hot
- Cold
- Jittery
- Fidgety
- Wiggly
- Sore
- Sweaty
- Cramped
- Itchy
- Tickly

Skill 3: Assess thoughts.

The Feelings Mind recognizes that emotions and body sensations are different from thoughts. For example, if a person is frustrated and their body feels tense, they may think: "breathe slowly, breathe slowly." Their thoughts in this scenario send a different message to their body and their emotions. In doing so, the person realizes that their Feelings Mind is open to feedback and that thinking can influence emotions. Without the insight and self-reflection of the Feelings Mind, individuals tend to react impulsively and lack full awareness and understanding of themselves in a situation. The change to recognizing and *thinking* about one's feelings without an immediate reaction may not happen right away, but with practice it can happen.

Skill 4: Acknowledge mood state.

The Feelings Mind recognizes if an emotion has been influenced by a particular mood. In other words, it discerns an underlying mood state such as depression, irritability, or optimism. When strong and consistent enough, a mood can influence feelings and their intensity. For example, when a teen is sad and insecure about their friendships, hopes for better connections, and feels disappointed or even depressed due to not being socially active, their mood state can influence their interactions with others and can color their emotions negatively. Someone may feel sadder than a given situation would warrant due to a depressed mood state.

Skill 5: Recognize mindset.

In close connection to understanding one's thinking, a Feelings Mind knows that a strong mindset can also influence feelings in a situation. Mindset is related to one's attitude and outlook. For example, if a person thinks about themselves in a generally negative manner, believing they are less worthy than others and possessing a low self-image, this mindset can influence their emotional reactions.

A more advanced Feelings Mind allows one to recognize their feelings as well as put them in perspective by understanding the variety of possible underlying reasons for them. Thoughts and feelings can be two different things. The advanced Feelings Mind knows that maintaining power over one's thoughts and behaviors can impact feelings. In addition, a person's values can influence their choices and feelings. When experiencing strong negative emotions, the Feelings Mind recognizes those emotions and understands that they do not have to drive behavior in a negative way.

When teaching the Feelings Mind, begin with the skill level that fits the person. Recognizing and labeling specific feelings is the first step. Differentiating them from body sensations and thoughts is the second layer of skill. Third, recognizing potential mood states or mindsets that may influence feelings will lead to the coping skill of how to influence one's emotions more effectively.

The Feelings Mind shows up when an individual:

- Tries to recognize and label their emotions.
- Tries to communicate their feelings.
- States or recognizes how their body feels.
- Recognizes their particular thoughts and differentiates those from feelings or behaviors.
- Identifies how they have been feeling over time and whether a consistent mood pattern exists.
- Recognizes how they think about a circumstance or issue, and can state their belief, impression, or perception.

Here are examples of the Feelings Mind:

- Liam did not get to play with his Nintendo Switch when he had to attend his sister's soccer game because his father said, "no, go run around and get some exercise." Liam expected to play on his Switch as he had been able to in the past. Besides, he didn't really need to see her play, did he? He became frustrated but was able to explain to his father that he was upset and disappointed because he thought he would be allowed to play, especially while waiting for the game to start and during halftime.

- Theresa noticed that she nitpicked her 9-year-old for her annoying habits—or what felt like annoying habits to her. In her own mind, Theresa recognized that she felt exhausted from the long day and week, due to work and home responsibilities, and apologized to her child for being grumpy and getting on her case more than necessary.

- Jasper was scheduled to give a speech in English class. As soon as she walked into the classroom, she noticed that her stomach felt queasy and her body began to tingle. She also recognized that she imagined freezing and forgetting what she had to say when giving her speech. She decided to take some deep breaths and visualize herself giving her speech just as she had practiced the night before in the mirror.

THE FEELINGS INVESTIGATOR

The Feelings Investigator's insights are similar to the Feelings Mind's. However, what differentiates these two Connectors is that the Feelings Investigator also understands the context of the situation including what may have precipitated it, the likely feelings of others within the same situation, and the perception of one's behavior within it.

The Feelings Investigator applies not only emotional intelligence to the situation but social intelligence too. To activate the Feelings Investigator within others, ask the following questions:

- How did you feel when that happened?
- How do you think this other person within the situation felt when that happened?
- Why do you think your feelings were the same or different?
- What was the most appropriate reaction in that situation (considering context and general expectations)?
- What would have made the situation turn out better or differently?

Common Skills of The Feelings Investigator

Skill 1: Recognize one's own feelings as well as the likely feelings of others.

The Feelings Investigator can recognize their feelings, the likely feelings of another, and the capacity of the specific situation to fuel emotion. The Feelings Investigator understands their own emotions within a context. They apply emotional and social intelligence to understand not only why one may feel or react a certain way, but also how the larger social context may affect the situation. They think about likely dynamics at play and are curious about them—thus the term "investigate." To understand emotional reactions within a larger context, the Feelings Investigator can utilize a variety of skills that include understanding the symptoms of big or intense feelings, identifying those feelings, determining if previous thoughts or feelings fueled emotions in the current situation, then also applying these skills when considering the feelings of others in the situation.

Skill 2: Assess the context, including what others expect and how the context may influence emotions.

The Feelings Investigator recognizes the nuances of what is behaviorally and socially expected in a given situation. For example, playful or teasing behavior may be funnier and more acceptable in one scenario than in another. One person may be more sensitive and react more negatively to certain types of teasing than another person, for their own specific reasons or because the teasing occurred in front of others and made them self-conscious. Many differing layers come into play when assessing a social context. Breaking down those layers and having insight into those components create greater social intelligence, and thus a strong Feelings Investigator.

Skill 3: Consider options in response.

The Feelings Investigator knows that there are options or choices in how to respond. Often, one responds based upon their emotions and how they feel within a situation. This can lead to reactionary responses. To take into consideration an array of choices and choose a wiser response, one's rational mind must work and think flexibly. A variety of responses or choices are often available. One must develop the skill to recognize what they are, which will then allow for a wise response.

Skill 4: Determine what would improve the situation for everyone.

This skill generally makes a person well liked. When one can see the different layers of the social and emotional context of a situation, as well as recognize that this context may not feel the same for everyone, then they can determine what may improve the situation. The Feelings Investigator knows how to explain what is happening, what to say to others to create more understanding, how to offer empathy when needed, and how to suggest solutions that are relevant and on target for all involved.

The Feelings Investigator shows up when an individual:

- Tries to understand how others feel.

- Recognizes that their feelings may be different from another person's in the same situation.

- Recognizes that there may be a larger consensus or common perception (for example, it is not okay to ask for a favor of someone when they are sad because they just lost their pet; compassion is the most appropriate response).

- Understands how others who observe the situation might perceive it.

- Knows that there is more than one way to think about a situation, whether outside or within one's own feelings, and more than one way to communicate these feelings.

- Develops and tries approaches to group understanding and communication.

- Communicates with a leadership that brings people to greater understanding and respect.

Examples of the Feelings Investigator

- Sami noticed that Desiree walked away when they were playing at recess. She didn't understand why, but wondered if Desiree might be upset about something. Sami noticed that Desiree's reactions were not typical and was curious and caring enough to ask why. Sami decided to go and ask Desiree if she was ok and why she left the game.

- Tamik's algebra teacher had been absent for three days due to illness. Tamik noticed that the class was loud and stressed while his teacher tried to answer questions and go over the study guide for the test that had been missed due to his absence. The class complained about the test; they felt it was rushed after working with a substitute for three days. Tamik decided to speak up and said, "Hey everyone, give Mr. Jones a break, he has been sick. He is a fair teacher; just give him a chance."

- Samuel's friends were hanging out at the coffee shop and got in a huge debate about politics. Samuel himself felt strongly about the topic being discussed. He was about to give his two cents because he was taught to speak his mind and believed his opinion needed to be heard as well. However, he stopped himself and instead said, "Guys, this is an important issue and we all feel strongly about it. But I don't want us to ruin our friendships over it, because we are not all going to agree on everything."

THE HELPFUL COACH

The Helpful Coach is a Connector that reminds a person to stop and take a breath. Instead of reacting to an intense emotion in the moment, the Helpful Coach recognizes that one needs to allow themselves—more specifically, their brain—a chance to think about what to do next.

This character helps people to communicate effectively and in a manner that is not impulsive or reactionary. The Helpful Coach also recognizes whether the situation, or its dynamic, may be too heated and calls a "time-out."

A fun way to present this character is to use the coach metaphor. Let's imagine a member of the team is frustrated, hurt, or angry; perhaps they feel like the game is not fair. The Helpful Coach knows there are other ways to play the game—smarter ways. He or she takes time to stop, think, and call a different play. The Helpful Coach notices their player getting increasingly upset and does not want to get a penalty. He or she wisely knows that time to "cool off" will get their player back on the right track.

Common Skills of the Helpful Coach

Skill 1: Recognize when to call a time-out.

The Helpful Coach knows when to stop and implement an effective break to regroup. They tell the other person they need a time-out, refrain from speaking, and then give themselves time to understand their feelings. Time-out activities include, for example, stopping to take a drink, going to a quiet space, doing something active to use up physical energy while thinking about what has happened, or using meditation or prayer.

Skill 2: Use positive motivation.

The Helpful Coach uses self-talk or discusses the situation with another person who can assist or inspire them in a positive way. Positive motivation relies on a mindset that helps a person believe that they can get through a situation capably and there can be some resolution. This skill helps a person let go of negative thinking within the situation and talk themselves down from anger and frustration.

Skill 3: Implement problem-solving.

The Helpful Coach knows that there are different ways to respond to any situation, even when upset or angry. Taking a time-out and calming oneself enough to think through different options or approaches is an important play. The Helpful Coach values a flexible mind. When one has little control over a situation, the Helpful Coach is able to implement problem-solving, think flexibly, and recognize the power and control one does have in the moment.

Skill 4: Ask for help.

During a "time-out," the Helpful Coach remembers that there are assistant coaches or people who may be there to listen, offer advice or ideas, and provide guidance when one feels stuck. Remembering to utilize support and being willing to accept it can help offset negative emotions. The Helpful Coach recognizes that when we cannot think of a productive solution, another trusted person can help.

The Helpful Coach shows up when an individual:

- Recognizes their feelings and knows that they need to calm down before responding.

- Communicates to others that they need a time-out.

- Uses strategies that allow for calming and clear thinking.

- Thinks flexibly in order to return to a situation productively.

- Asks for help from an adult or others when they recognize they are stuck in their thinking.

Examples of the Helpful Coach

- Jace was about to yell in Andre's face for calling the ball "out" when it was obviously in. Jace was convinced that Andre only wanted to win and wasn't being fair. It was all Jace could take. However, he had a brief glimmer of a thought that if he blew up at Andre, he would get in trouble. So he walked off, even though others said, "What are you doing?" Jace had to get himself out of the situation before he really went off on Andre.

- Juan was fed up with his sister always getting her way. He felt certain that their mother gave her favorable treatment and always saw things his sister's way, not his. Now it was happening again: he wanted to sit in the front seat and his sister said it was her turn. They began to argue, when their mother said in an agitated tone, "Do I need to get involved between you two again?!" Juan did not want that to happen, because he was sure it wouldn't go his way. His mother would side with his sister again, of course. So, instead, he decided just to take a deep breath, let it go, and talk to his mother about it later.

- Allison's boyfriend said that he would not meet her tomorrow as planned because something else had come up. Allison didn't know what had happened but felt quite mad because he was ditching her. She was about to text back and tell him how rude he was and to "just forget it." However, she stopped herself, erased the reactionary text, and decided to give him a chance—maybe there was a reasonable explanation. Either way, she didn't want to say something she would later regret.

SHOES

The Connector character Shoes considers trying to stand in someone else's experience. This character is an illustration of the saying, "Try to walk a mile in someone else's shoes." Shoes stops to wonder whether the other person has a different experience and consequently, whether they may have a different emotional reaction in a given situation. Shoes is curious about wanting to understand the other person's feelings.

SHOES

This character is important within relationships because it helps a person take the time to give a caring response. This leads to communication and understanding of another person's perspective and thus ultimately increases connection.

Common Skills of Shoes

Skill 1: Understand that others have their own internal experience.

The first step for Shoes is to realize that another person's feelings are not the same as their own. This is especially important when one feels something very strongly. In these moments, Shoes helps a person to stop and try to understand why another person feels their own emotions and has a different experience.

Skill 2: Acknowledge that others have different life experiences.

Life experiences are different from internal experiences in that they are external. The events and situations that happen to each person over their lifespan are unique and play a large role in creating that person's unique internal experience. It is important to recognize that one person's life experiences are not the same as another's and may influence their emotions and reactions.

Skill 3: Recognize that another person's experiences may cause them to react differently.

Shoes recognizes that different internal and external experiences influence a person's reactions, feelings, and expectations. This can help us to understand the source of another's thinking and perspective, or least part of it. While we may not always agree with another person's perspective, we can at least try to understand it and its origin.

Skill 4: Seek to understand another person's experience through evidence or active listening.

Caring about how another feels or experiences a situation is essential to connection. This can be done very simply ("yeah, I get it") or in a more detailed manner, in a more robust conversation. Either way, the act and intention of "getting it" and showing enough caring to "get it" are some of the most important skills that Shoes has to offer. This includes being able to ask another person why they feel or react the way they do, while caring about their experiences. This skill requires patience, even when feeling uncomfortable or disagreeing with the other person. Acknowledging that they have been heard and understood makes a huge connection.

Shoes shows up when an individual:

- Recognizes that others have unique feelings and perceptions.
- Comprehends that each person may have a different experience, even in the same situation.
- Seeks to understand the other person's feelings or experiences and respond accordingly.
- Uses active listening skills.

Examples of Shoes

- Mrs. Graves was about to go into a parent meeting with the father of one of her students. She suspected that he was upset with her over his son's grade. She felt nervous about meeting with him because parents can be quite defensive and easily upset when it comes to their child struggling. She realized this was probably the primary thing to remember when meeting with this parent. If she could convey that she understood his feelings and try to work with him to help this student, then the conversation would likely be more productive. Being a parent herself, she knew how to mentally put herself in the parent perspective.

- Jessa had just colored her hair and felt a little insecure about how it looked. Her close friend Izzy was first to see it and said, "Wow, that is different!" Jessa immediately interpreted this as a negative comment and spouted off, "Well, I realize that I cannot afford to go the salon, but you don't have to be so rude! Thanks a lot, Izzy!" Izzy was able to keep her cool. She understood that Jessa was often sensitive, especially about her looks. Izzy said, "Jessa, I didn't mean anything negative about your hair. I just meant that it looks very different now, not that it looks bad. It just makes you look different than before—in a good way."

- Jason and Sara got in a big fight. They were not speaking and stood at a stalemate, each convinced that the other needed to apologize. Their best friend said, "Hey you two, you are going to have to listen to each other. The only way to figure this out is to hear what the other has to say, be patient, and then state your feelings as well. That's what it takes to be in a relationship. You have to understand where the other is coming from and be willing to listen to them in order to move forward."

Two-Way Street

Two-Way Street understands that people have different perspectives. While similar to Shoes, this Connector focuses on thinking and less on feelings. Two-Way Street acknowledges that another person may be coming from a different perspective than themselves and seeks to understand how.

Two-Way Street is willing to respect a different perspective, even if they strongly disagree, and to see how things look from the other side of the street, even if it does not fully make sense to them. Understanding and respect are both required to create more connection.

Common Skills of Two-Way Street

Skill 1: Recognize that others have different thoughts, opinions, and perspectives.

Two-Way Street is a skill that requires recognizing that one's thoughts are different from another person's. Two-Way Street grasps that people can hold different perspectives and opinions about certain events.

Skill 2: Show willingness to understand another's perspective.

A second component of Two-Way Street is a willingness to remain open to another's perspective. Discounting another's perspective can be easy, but developing a patient understanding that each person possesses a unique perspective (often based on their experiences and feelings) and is worthy of understanding, creates more connection.

Skill 3: Acknowledge and respect another's perspective.

A willing attitude to respect a different perspective or opinion, even if not agreeing with it, is another skill of Two-Way Street. This character offers an openness to another's perspective, even in the face of conflict. Showing respect to another when believing they are in error allows for more connection than discounting, ignoring, or even admonishing a different perspective.

Skill 4: Accept that group perspectives exist and differ.

Two-Way Street acknowledges that differences exist between social groups. For example a small group of friends may have a different perspective than another small group of friends, teachers can have a different perspective than students, or parents will have a different perspective than their children. Treating others who may have a different perspective with respect can allow for more open dialogue and understanding as opposed to disconnection.

Two-Way Street shows up when an individual:

- Recognizes that others have their own unique thoughts and perspectives.

- Understands that there are reasons behind others' perspectives and shows willingness to try and understand another's perspective.

- Treats another's perspective with respect, even if not fully understanding or agreeing with it.

- Recognizes group perspectives and tries to understand them and their origin.

Examples of Two-Way Street

- Silas was very upset that his teacher took his favorite fidget toy. He couldn't believe that she would do that, especially because last year's teacher didn't seem to mind, and neither did his classmates. When he told his father, his father said, "Silas, it is important to understand that what is okay with one teacher may not be okay with another teacher. Your new teacher may find it distracting, think you are not listening, or believe that it is distracting other students, even if you do not. In other words, her perspective is not the same as yours."

- Josie became very angry with her friend Brie who kept talking to the new girl at lunch and seemed to want to find out everything about her. Josie felt left out. After lunch, Brie told Josie that she herself had been the "new kid" before and that she wanted to make the new student feel welcome. Josie then understood that Brie's thought process was about allowing someone else to feel comfortable, not trying to exclude her.

- It dawned on Charles that Roberto's perspective on racial inclusion was likely different than his, based upon their backgrounds and experiences. Therefore, he decided to ask Roberto what he thought and what would make their current situation more inclusive.

Captain Courageous

Captain Courageous reminds a person that managing conflict in a healthy way is important for connection. This character thinks about how to move beyond one's upset feelings and sees that the particular issue upsetting them is probably not more important than their relationships.

Captain Courageous allows a person to identify their feelings, needs, and thoughts, and to let down their defenses. It allows a person to be open, honest, and vulnerable, and even admit when they are wrong. Captain Courageous seeks connection through honest self-reflection, cares about both self and others, admits their deeper feelings, and acknowledges their role in situations, including when there are misunderstandings. The term "courageous" is used because all of these skills require courage, even in close relationships. When Captain Courageous shows up with trusted others, it can be powerful for the person and their relationships.

Common Skills for Captain Courageous

Skill 1: Let down defenses.

Letting down defenses is a huge step for Captain Courageous, since defenses allow individuals to protect themselves. One should not ignore circumstances when one may need to protect themselves, but within important and trusting relationships, letting down defenses can create a truer reflection of one's deepest and most heartfelt self. Captain Courageous tears down the emotional wall that keeps one from being vulnerable and compassionate.

Defenses may show up as the following:

- Denying that there is anything wrong or that one has feelings about a situation.

- Stating that something is "not a big deal" and trying to avoid addressing something that is impactful.

- Lashing out at others when feeling disappointed or upset.

- Blaming others for a situation or one's own feelings.

- Avoiding addressing the situation by various means as long as it delays having to address it.

- Acting like the other person has a problem.

- Changing the subject.

- Behaving aggressively verbally or physically.

- Assuming that nothing good or helpful will come if the situation is addressed.

Skill 2: Practice humility.

Captain Courageous shows up when a person is self-reflective and able to see their role in situations and to be honest about their intentions. It allows a person to admit when they are wrong and be open to sharing. Practicing humility includes being able to admit and/or apologize if someone has been hurt, whether on purpose or by accident.

Skill 3: Communicate effectively.

This skill includes sharing one's feelings and engaging in mutual communication. Captain Courageous recognizes when communication takes the form of an argument or when one or both parties only try to articulate their points. Captain Courageous works toward two-way communication, which includes both sharing and listening.

Skill 4: Maintain a caring attitude even when hurt, angered, or upset.

This skill promotes working through difficult moments, as well as through disappointed, hurt, or angry feelings. It includes allowing oneself to care about another person even if hurt by them. Captain Courageous understands one's own feelings, recognizes one's role in a situation, communicates what is needed, and maintains a caring attitude about a relationship, themselves, and the other person involved. When conflict occurs with a person close to them, who cares about them, and with whom they have a generally healthy relationship, Captain Courageous puts caring over anger and hurt. If the relationship has value, even if not a very close relationship, Captain Courageous can still do all of the above for the betterment of all involved. Captain Courageous cares about others, even if they do something that is hurtful, whether intentionally or inadvertently. (Note: Captain Courageous does not apply to any response to abusive behaviors, when one is humiliated, harmed, or systematically mistreated. Emotional, behavioral, and psychological responses to any form of abuse are not included within this system and should be addressed therapeutically.)

Captain Courageous shows up when an individual:

- Admits wrongdoing or the role they have played in a situation.
- Recognizes when the relationship is more important than an argument, disagreement, or disappointment.
- Respects others even when they disagree or do not see an issue in the same way.
- Communicates their understanding of the situation and finds ways to bring about peace and respect within the relationship.
- Ultimately maintains a caring perspective and attitude.

Examples of Captain Courageous

- Mallory knew that Francie's feelings had been hurt. She didn't really understand why or what she had done. However, she did not want something to get in the way of their friendship, so she asked Francie to talk after school. She hoped that Francie could share her feelings without getting upset, defensive, or accusatory, so that they could both leave feeling better about their relationship. Mallory had taken a courageous first step and hoped for the best.

- When Mallory and Francie met, Francie was mad at Mallory for being so insensitive and leaving her out of her weekend plans. She felt totally dissed by Mallory and made it clear that she felt Mallory was mean to her. Mallory was taken off guard: she did not see it that way, nor did she intentionally hurt Francie. She felt that spending time with another friend was perfectly okay and that Francie had herself done that. Given Francie's accusatory tone, Mallory wanted to go off on her but decided that it wasn't worth it. In the big picture, Francie was hurt and felt left out. Ultimately she wanted to feel like the two were good friends and that their friendship had not changed. So instead Mallory said, "Francie, I still think that you are my best friend, but I believe that it is okay to spend time with other friends too. I feel that our friendship is strong enough that we can spend time with others, and I hope that you do too."

- Francie still felt hurt but accepted what Mallory said. Later that night, when she talked to her mom about it, she decided that although she felt insecure about Mallory's other friendship, she knew that handling her insecurity was important in order to maintain a healthy relationship with Mallory. She texted Mallory that she understood and was glad that they could talk about hard things, which only made their friendship stronger.

Mending in Action

Mending in Action is an extension of Captain Courageous in that this character actively engages in repairing a relationship that has been damaged by actions, hurt feelings, misunderstandings, or arguments.

Mending in Action represents the conscious effort of healing what has been hurt so that future interactions become less awkward, avoidant, or resentful. It requires all of Captain Courageous's skills as well as an honest intention for a positive relationship. Mending in Action realizes the importance of taking active steps to improve a relationship or a given situation.

Common Skills of Mending In Action

Skill 1: Use communication that reconciles and seeks to bring peace.

This includes intentional word choices as well as verbal or nonverbal communication that leads to repairing hurt or misunderstanding. Mending in Action is non-threatening in approach and allows others to feel safe or calm in their presence.

Skill 2: Show compassion and respect to others.

Mending in Action displays intentional actions that are kind and caring, or even loving in close relationships. This character demonstrates genuine efforts to be respectful to others and oneself, and to bring kindness into the situation.

Skill 3: Engage in repair such as apologies and a willingness to listen.

This skill seeks to understand, communicate in a fair and balanced way, and recognize when apologies are needed. Mending in Action may ask why someone is hurt if they do not know, apologize if they have had a role in the problem, and show compassion toward another person. This is most effective when both parties participate.

Skill 4: Commit to a different path in the future.

Mending in Action takes steps to understand and commits to avoiding a similar hurtful experience or misunderstanding in the future. This skill speaks to learning from situations and developing a deeper understanding of how to move forward without repeating problematic behaviors. It is best accomplished by naming a specific behavior or action that will replace a hurtful one.

Mending in Action shows up when an individual:

- Communicates compassion, understanding, and a willingness to repair hurt feelings.
- Shares their own thoughts and feelings in a respectful manner to both parties.
- Takes steps to improve relationships.
- Accepts responsibility for their part in a situation.
- Works to communicate in a balanced way, understanding both sides.

Examples of Mending in Action:

- Xavier sent flowers to his girlfriend as a gesture of apology after they had a big fight. They had seen her ex-boyfriend at the football game the previous night, which caused Xavier to feel very jealous, and consequently lose his temper and say things that he regretted.
- Collin hugs his mother and says "I'm sorry" after he yelled at her for trying to help him. He knows that she was doing her best. He was irritated at something that had happened earlier in the day and took it out on her.
- Gabby told her brother that she was sorry she was busy and didn't listen to him when he was upset. She promised she wanted to listen to him now and vowed to do better in the future.

Healthy Tools

We use various tools to assist us with connection. These Connector tools can be broken down into simple components and considered individually, especially when one particular tool can help in a given situation or be used with other tools to bring calmer responses and greater connection.

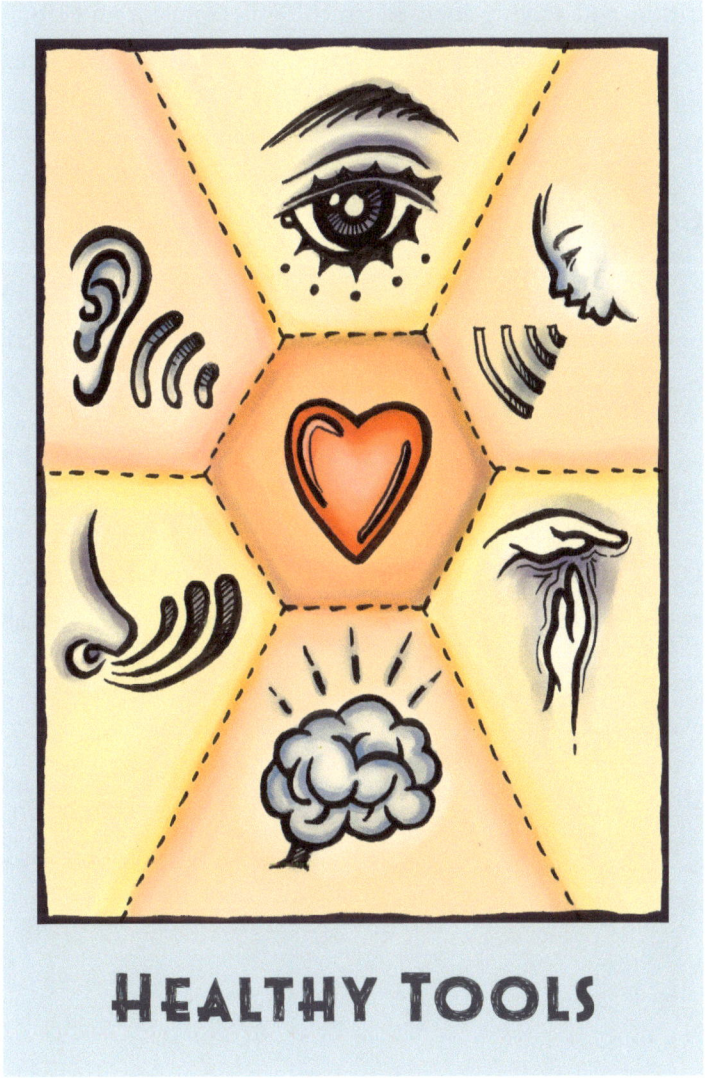

Healthy Tools

Tool 1: Heart

The Heart reminds us that one cares about relationships and others, even when mad, upset, or disappointed.

Tool 2: Eyes

Using one's Eyes can assist connection by making eye contact during respectful communication and staying focused on the other person and situation. Eyes can also notice another person's facial expressions and body language, which can help in trying to understand how they feel.

Tool 3: Connecting Voice

When using a Connecting Voice, one uses their words and tone in order to improve the situation. This requires maintaining a calm and respectful tone as opposed to a rude or agitated one.

Tool 4: Stop and Think (Time-Out)

Before reacting out of strong emotion, we can Stop and Think about the best response, or at least a response that is not impulsive or later regrettable.

Tool 5: Thinking Brain

This tool reminds us to recognize the presence of our Thinking Brain and use it even in the face of strong emotions. It leads a person to think prior to making impulsive decisions and formulate a more productive response.

Tool 6: Breath

Breath has the power to calm one's body and mind. When recognized and utilized appropriately, it can assist us in using our Thinking Brain as well as managing intense emotions in a given moment.

Tool 7: Power to Listen and Share

Actively listening to what another person has to say, then reflecting it back to them is a terrific and effective tool to build understanding and respect. It is an advanced skill, in that it requires understanding and managing one's own feelings while being able to fully listen to another's feelings, which may conflict with your own.

CHAPTER 5

MEET THE DISCONNECTORS

Disconnectors are a group of characters who, when they feel emotions in a situation, express frustration, irritation, and anger. The Disconnectors tend to withdraw or fight, but do not engage in a way that brings resolve. When emotions fuel a reaction, one may not recognize all perspectives, understand the entirety of their own feelings, or think about problem solving. The Disconnectors are stuck in their mindset or emotion, so they react in ways that perpetuate these feelings, thereby not allowing a broader understanding of themselves, the situation, or others. Their reactions disconnect them from others. Disconnectors typically work hard to get what they want in the moment, but do not recognize or consistently respect how this may impact others, their relationships, or themselves in the long term. Each Disconnector will be described in detail in this chapter and they are presented in this order: Fighter, Deflector, Insulator, No Way, Grumpmeister, and One-Way Street, as well as Defenses.

To access a pdf version of all Disconnector images, go to:
http://www.tishtaylor.com/Disconnectors/pdf

Meet the Disconnectors

Disconnector	Behaviors	Common Responses to the Disconnector
Fighter	1. Wounding Words 2. The Strike 3. The Inflator 4. The Barrage	1. Defensiveness 2. Surrender 3. Harsh Punishment
Deflector	1. Denial 2. Blame 3. Argument	1. Debate 2. Frustration 3. Surrender
Insulator	1. Cocooning 2. Isolation 3. Deflection	1. Confusion 2. Coaxing 3. Frustration
No Way	1. Ignoring 2. Postponement 3. Refusal	1. Coercion 2. Punishment 3. Yelling
Grumpmeister	1. Visible Irritation 2. Negative Responses 3. Inaction	1. Placating 2. Cheerleading 3. Avoidance
One-Way Street	1. Inflexible Responses 2. Irritation 3. Apparent Stubbornness	1. Arguing 2. Exasperation 3. Avoidance

The Fighter

The Fighter enters a situation on guard, ready to defend their position or argue their point without seeing or considering the broader perspective. They only consider their feelings or thoughts, which are typically narrow in scope. This Disconnector often feels disappointed or frustrated.

They think things are unfair, and, at times, they attack the person they see as the culprit instigating their frustration or anger. They tend to argue or fight with the person on whom they can most easily take their negative feelings out—typically a person close to them. The Fighter often breaks relationship rules by fighting unfairly or in a way in which no one wins, but feels victory in the short term ("I was right"; "You hurt me, so I am going to hurt you"; "You need to be told why you are wrong").

The Fighter often doesn't have full insight into their feelings, which may include disappointment as well as frustration. They may not recognize that they project onto another person a variety of feelings that have culminated into anger. The Fighter child often ends up in trouble with adults. The Fighter teen or adult typically experiences strained relationships. Once these interactions are over, those involved can feel battle-worn.

The Fighter uses many defenses and weapons to hold their position, fight for what they want, or attack in ways they feel are warranted in the moment.

Common Behaviors of The Fighter

Behavior 1: Wounding Words

The Fighter may say things that are personal and hurtful or try to make the other person feel as bad as they do. Using Wounding Words can make the other person hurt the same way the Fighter does. Wounding words can also create a sense of power over the other person, by attacking them for what they have done, even if the perceived transgression is exaggerated.

Behavior 2: The Strike

The Fighter may use the Strike to lash out at the person with whom they are upset, who has made them angry or frustrated, or who they feel treated them unfairly. For example, reminding them of a painful regret from their past or destroying something important to them.

Behavior 3: The Inflator

The Inflator occurs when The Fighter determines to get back at the person who has hurt or upset them in a bigger way than how they were hurt or disappointed. This assumed position of power makes them feel stronger in the moment. Negative defenses take over because the Fighter attempts to be stronger and tougher.

Behavior 4: The Barrage

The Barrage is another position of power, but expressed in a negative, overpowering manner. There is little to no chance of rational response to a barrage.

What Do the above Behaviors Accomplish?

In the moment, they can accomplish a release of strong emotions. At times, they may reflect a previous buildup of emotion, which also speaks to a lack of internal understanding, of prior communication, and often of impulse control. These behaviors may also create a sense of power for The Fighter when they feel as if they have been treated wrongly or unfairly.

The person receiving The Fighter's blasting behaviors becomes a participant in the disconnection that occurs. While the person in Fighter mode generates their own negativity and disconnection, their behavior creates disconnection in the other person as well—in some ways similar.

Common responses to The Fighter include:

Response 1: Defensiveness

The person on the receiving end attempts to argue back, stick up for themselves, debate the point, or yell back so that it is not a one-sided attack without a fight. Many times, this can strengthen The Fighter in both individuals.

Response 2: Surrender

The other person may give in because it is too hard to argue, fight back, or be rational. They may concede the point in an effort to stop the negative interaction or arguments, but the truth is that they feel the opposite or differently. This can lead to resentment and disconnection.

Response 3: Harsh Punishment

Parents may tend to strongly punish Fighter behavior in the moment (or threaten harsh punishment) in order to gain control and make it clear that the behavior is unacceptable.

After an interaction with The Fighter, most people end up feeling angry, hurt, or upset. These occurrences often require repair, or they may leave scorched earth that must eventually be overcome in some way. The more frequently The Fighter shows up, the more disconnection occurs between individuals.

Examples of The Fighter:

- Sam yells at his mother when she asks him to complete his homework before playing video games. He becomes immediately angered and screams at her, "You must be an idiot if you think I don't know that!"

- William kicks his younger brother because he has borrowed (or "taken," according to William) a piece from William's Lego set to use for a structure that he is making. William is very mad because he believes that his brother took it on purpose, always takes his things, and deserves this reaction.

- Samantha vehemently argues with her friend over who is right. Samantha believes that her friend was rude and left her out of the weekend plans for a sleepover. Samantha insists that she is correct, continues to argue her points, and will not let her friend get a word in to explain her side of the story.

Tips for when The Fighter shows up:

- Slow the interaction down and try not to react quickly. Notice who is showing up and understand the person is in this specific Fighter mindset, which is fueled by a lack of perspective or understanding, emotional dysregulation, or lack of emotional control. (See: The Helpful Coach)

- Create more physical space between yourself and The Fighter. It is more difficult to intensify interactions when physically distanced from someone who is angry and hurtful. (See: Healthy Tools—Thinking Brain and Breath)

- Use careful listening skills to calm The Fighter down. Let them know that you want to understand what they are upset about and what is underneath their emotion. Again, this requires slowing down the interaction, repeating back what they are saying, and making sure that they feel understood. (See: Shoes and Two-Way Street)

The Deflector

The Deflector is not willing or able to acknowledge their part in a situation. The Deflector blames others for the situation as well as for their own behavior. They find various reasons for their behavior, which others view as excuses. The Deflector presents as strong and willful. They may be reacting this way for different reasons: shame, feeling very insecure, or feeling upset with themselves on a deeper level.

Conversely, smugness may fuel The Deflector, as the person may feel convinced and confident that they are right. Either way, The Deflector does not accept responsibility.

The Deflector uses many behaviors to repel or avert their responsibility or their role in a situation. These include the following:

Common Behaviors of The Deflector

Behavior 1: Denial

This sounds like "it's not my fault." The Deflector is not willing to consider or hear how another person might have experienced their behavior or actions. They may even do something as physical and obvious as put their hands over their ears and refuse to listen.

Behavior 2: Blame

Blaming the other person is a common defense of The Deflector. This occurs when they insist that the other person is at fault, and not them. They may admit the behavior, but state that the other person caused them to do it. This still avoids any responsibility for their own choices in the interaction or the situation.

Behavior 3: Argument

The Deflector will argue their point, including the facts or details of the interaction. They will insist they are right and the other person is wrong. The Deflector will avoid honestly listening to another as they feel it is more important to be right and show the other person why. They can hone their argument to a level that makes two-way communication difficult.

In these moments, The Deflector does not seem to care about how others feel, but only about how they themselves are not wrong or "bad." They may want to win or come out on top of the situation, which means making it the other person's fault or issue. This behavior may indicate a fragile ego or an inability to see larger and different perspectives.

Common Responses to The Deflector

Response 1: Debate

The other person states their position in order to show The Deflector what they need to acknowledge and why. This tends to become a back-and-forth communication that creates frustration because the Deflector is unwilling to recognize their role.

Response 2: Frustration

Frustration occurs quickly with The Deflector because, while the adult works to teach The Deflector another way to think or perceive the situation, The Deflector denies or shifts responsibility. Frustrations can also rise up because The Deflector seems to be stubborn and refuses to accept their role.

Response 3: Surrender

Parents or adults may eventually surrender as the argument or debate is not fruitful. When it seems that The Deflector is unwilling to accept responsibility, it can end in exasperation.

Examples of The Deflector

- When Travis was asked why he didn't take the trash out for the weekly trash pickup, he immediately said: "It's your fault for not reminding me."

- Benjamin refused to hear or acknowledge that he had any part in getting an infraction at school. He insisted that the teacher "is mean" and that he did not do anything wrong. He would not have an infraction if she were nicer.

- Kimberly was very tired and ended up being late for school. She reported to her father that she just couldn't sleep well and therefore found it too difficult to wake up on time. She omitted that she had been up on Snapchat until midnight.

Tips for When the Deflector Shows Up

- Think about the cost versus benefit of getting into the argument. Is the argument worth it? You may state your point or what may need to be said, but an ongoing debate over who is right or wrong is a road that leads to frustration and anger. You could simply state, "I do not want to argue. We can agree to disagree." (See: Healthy Tools—Thinking Brain and Connecting Voice)

- Use language that encourages increased perspective such as, "I know that we both have strong feelings about what has happened" or "I can see that you are upset. I know that I am upset too, but for different reasons." This language inserts the idea that there is more than one perspective of the situation and encourages movement away from an inflexible viewpoint. (See: Two-Way Street, Feelings Investigator, and Healthy Tools—Power to Listen and Share)

- Recognize your own feelings in the situation and try not to react to frustration and anger. Utilize a more rational approach or take a time-out if The Deflector is unable to be flexible or accept anything other than their own point of view. Come back to the topic when all are calmer. (See: Feelings Mind and Helpful Coach)

The Insulator

The Insulator is unable to accept anyone's help in the moment. This Disconnector refuses to hear any constructive feedback or listen to what is being said to them, especially if it involves their behavior. The Insulator just wants to be left alone.

The Insulator is a close relative of The Deflector but differs in that The Insulator appears emotionally overwhelmed and presents like they cannot handle the situation. (The Deflector may also be emotionally overwhelmed but appears more willful and demonstrates strong behaviors that deflect blame.)

The Insulator often shows up when a person believes that they are not understood or heard. They typically feel intense emotions that vary in nature, which increases their sense of overwhelm. There can be a combination of frustration, anger, disappointment, stress, sadness, guilt, shame, and possibly even despair. In this state, the Insulator has stopped any effective listening as they are just trying to deal with their own emotional state.

The Insulator can also become a default mode when a person becomes mad, frustrated, or overwhelmed. They may feel that certain situations keep coming up and feel powerless to change this pattern, so they default to overwhelm fueled by hopelessness.

The Insulator's behaviors are typically noticeable, since their level of emotional overwhelm is palpable in the moment.

Common Behaviors of The Insulator

Behavior 1: Cocooning

The Insulator can visibly isolate themselves in order to be left alone. This obvious physical retreat can include covering their ears, trying to block other people from talking to them, or huddling in a ball to avoid attempts at interaction.

Behavior 2: Isolation

The Insulator commonly does their best to get away or separate themselves from other people in the interaction. This includes walking away or leaving the situation.

Behavior 3: Deflection

Behaviors that deflect interaction can appear in different forms. They include yelling or getting very angry in order to be left alone, as well as making statements such as "I can't hear you" to irritate the other person and stop them from engaging.

While the Insulator appears unwilling to listen or problem-solve, they may in turn feel that the other person is unwilling to listen and problem-solve. Thus, they feel stuck. Showing up as The Insulator hinders problem-solving and emotional management. Encountering The Insulator can become frustrating, as it can appear that they do not care.

Common Responses to The Insulator

Response 1: Confusion

The Insulator's behavior can leave a person unsure how to respond. Is it anger, overwhelm, stubbornness, or all of them combined? Because The Insulator's emotional state appears fragile, knowing how to respond is difficult.

Response 2: Coaxing

A common response is to try and coax The Insulator into a more amenable mindset. This usually entails trying to reason with The Insulator.

Response 3: Frustration

The Insulator's intense reaction can quickly spark frustration in the other person, often leading to yelling or arguing. This causes The Insulator to retreat even further into isolation or a highly emotional state.

Examples of The Insulator

- Pam ran to her room, slammed the door, and shouted "I don't want to talk about it!" when her mother tried to ask her about why she has been so upset lately.

- Spencer continued to escalate as he attempted to finish a difficult math assignment—or at least what appeared to be a difficult math assignment to him. He showed visible frustration by crumpling his paper and slamming his pencil down, and eventually tucked his head into his knees and cried, refusing to return to the assignment.

- Amanda has had a very difficult time with her middle school friends. She has been upset lately following some negative comments about her on social media. She knows that she is being left out of plans with her friends because they seem to be annoyed or upset with her. She doesn't know what she has done to make them this upset. She doesn't want to talk about it and just goes to her room, shuts the door, and watches YouTube.

Tips for When The Insulator Shows Up

- Demonstrate a caring and respectful attitude with a simple and conciliatory statement such as "I do want to work this out with you" or "Your feelings are important in this situation." This effort can hopefully help the person feel cared for, which is often needed for them to address a situation while big emotions are present. (See: Healthy Tools—Heart and Connecting Voice)

- Communicate to The Insulator that you are willing to work through the problem or help them solve their problem. This may sound like "I would like to help you" or "I do want us to listen to each other." Be willing to sit with their emotions as they try or at least begin to communicate. (See: Captain Courageous)

- Use humor or another way to lighten the situation that would be meaningful to that person. This may include an inside joke, a particular event that you know both of you can laugh about, or a funny face or voice that is typically humorous to the person. (See: Feelings Investigator)

No Way

No Way shows up with a definitive attitude that communicates "I am not going to do what you say." The clear message is that this Disconnector rejects the other person's direction or request. No Way typically has a quick "no" response and can show very mild to intense refusals and behavior. This may include not stopping to consider the request or its consequences.

Often No Way's reaction allows the person to retain some personal power, for example with a "you can't make me" attitude. Their response often suggests inflexibility. The adult or whoever is giving a direction or expectation must then determine how they will respond to a direct refusal.

No Way can be a very frustrating Disconnector for parents or persons in an authority role. With certain children or individuals, moving past this stance is workable if you are able to address what may be stressing them or upsetting them. In these instances, the refusal may be related to feeling overwhelmed or stressed, or feeling that too much is being asked of them. In certain individuals, the No Way character tends to be more frequent as they seek to maintain their sense of control, do not want to be told what to do, and are comfortable refusing directions or expectations. This behavior can be heightened at certain developmental levels, but is also more frequent with certain individuals, such as those with Oppositional Defiant Disorder.

Common Behaviors of No Way

Behavior 1: Ignoring

No Way may act as if they do not hear direction or instructions. They seem focused on something else as they refuse to acknowledge what is asked or stated.

Behavior 2: Postponement

A common response by No Way aims to delay interaction, like "I'll do it in a minute." This leads to avoidance or non-compliance, because No Way does not deem the task important at that time—or at all. This behavior postpones a reaction and gets the adult "off their back" for a period of time.

Behavior 3: Refusal

This is a direct and clear refusal to follow a request. It sounds like "no, I won't do that" or simply "no."

These No Way responses leave an adult quite frustrated, especially if No Way is a common behavior pattern and style of response. Many parents and adults are left to find other means of responding to No Way behaviors as it can lead to negative interactions quite quickly.

Common Responses to No Way

Response 1: Coercion

A typical response to No Way is to tell them what will happen if they refuse to comply. This includes threatened consequences that tend to be large—possibly extreme—and quite meaningful to the teen or child. These consequences tend to spur a power struggle between the adult and No Way. If the teen or child ultimately does not comply, the balance of power may feel uncertain.

Response 2: Punishment

In response to No Way, the adult actually gives a punishment or consequence. These punishments often cannot be followed through as they are reactionary and threatened in the moment without much forethought.

Response 3: Yelling

Getting louder in order to gain control of the situation is a common response to No Way. It occurs out of frustration and may add to the power struggle.

Examples of No Way

- Baron is playing video games. His mother tells him that his time is up and that he needs to turn it off or finish the game. He purposely ignores her and continues to play, not intending to end his game nor turn it off when it is over.

- Fernando kicks his sister hard. He is angry at her for her comment about his shoes, which he perceived as rude. His mother gets upset and says,

"You cannot do that!" But Fernando continues to kick her as he believes she deserves it for being rude to him (after all this is a pattern of hers, according to him). He ignores his mother's direction to "stop that now!"

- Brittany's 7th grade English teacher assigns an in-class essay for today's class. Brittany does not want to do it, feels that it will be too much work, and decides that she will not do it. Instead she sits in her seat and pretends to be working, even though she has no intention of beginning the essay.

Tips for When No Way Shows Up

- Recognize if something about the direction or request is causing stress or overwhelm. If so, try to communicate and problem-solve with the child or teen to determine how to cope with what is asked of them. For example, "Is something about this hard?" "Can you tell me why you do not want to do this?" You may find a reason for the behavior which can be addressed and may not have been understood without asking. (See: Feelings Investigator and Shoes)

- When a child or teen actively refuses your direction or request, recognize your feelings as an adult or authority figure. Often when we feel disrespected, we can react quickly or rashly, which may lead to a power struggle when the child or teen refuses an important direction. Instead, respond from a place that recognizes "who is showing up" in the behavior, and proceed with appropriate and pre-determined consequences to the situation if the child or teen refuses to change their behavior. (See: Feelings Mind)

- Wait it out. At times, a No Way appearance will turn into compliance if the response to the refusal is more casual, gently persistent, or direct and expectant. This may sound like, "OK, I will give you a minute to see if you change your mind." "All right, I know you do not want to do this, but I have given you a minute and now it is time." This is accompanied with a calm voice and expectant and understanding tone. (See: Healthy Tools—Thinking Brain and Connecting Voice)

Grumpmeister

Grumpmeister shows up irritated, impatient, and annoyed. Grumpmeister tends to pick on others and find fault in them or blame others for their feelings. This Disconnector brings all-around irritability to the situation, making interactions more difficult.

Grumpmeister finds fault or difficulty in details and loses sight of the most important aspect of the situation. For example, when a child shows up as Grumpmeister in the morning, they are difficult to wake up, may yell or complain at their parent, or refuse to get ready for the day. Grumpmeister often lacks insight into their mood and sees external circumstances as being the reason for their feelings. Grumpmeister tends to work in conjunction with other Disconnectors such as The Deflector, which feeds upon their negative feelings and mood and their lack of willingness or insight into themselves.

Grumpmeister can be triggered by various things, but this behavior typically begins with feeling irritable, sad, disappointed, or dejected in some way. This in turn makes things all around seem more unfair, unpleasant, or irritating. Their negativity can be directed at themselves as well as others. This Disconnector may feel negatively about themselves and turn on themselves, including stating what is wrong with them as a person. Interacting with Grumpmeister requires patience, understanding, and fortitude.

Common Behaviors of Grumpmeister

Behavior 1: Visible Irritation

Grumpmeister is quite noticeable as the person demonstrates irritability in their facial expression, tone of voice, and body gestures. Other telltales signs may be low frustration tolerance and limited patience.

Behavior 2: Negative Responses

Grumpmeister perceives situations or circumstances as negative in general. This includes the other person's interaction with them and the feeling that something is not fair or right about the situation. This behavior usually sidelines progress as Grumpmeister becomes stuck in their way of thinking.

Behavior 3: Inaction

This Disconnector has low motivation for simple tasks or expectations. Their irritable mood makes even simple, everyday tasks difficult.

Common responses to Grumpmeister

Response 1: Placating

The adult or other person finds themselves "walking on eggshells" around Grumpmeister. They often try to please the teen or child or remove potential irritations so the situation does not worsen.

Response 2: Cheerleading

A cheering response can be common, in order to try and get Grumpmeister into a better mood. The adult hopes that their positivity can transfer or encourage Grumpmeister.

Response 3: Avoidance

The adult may choose not to engage or ask anything of this Disconnector in hopes that they will come around in time. In this "wait it out" approach, the adult concludes that nothing productive will happen with the Grumpmeister's state of mind.

If Grumpmeister shows up often or consistently, determining if an underlying issue exists (other than being grumpy at the situation) is important. This may include assessing whether an underlying mood issue is at play, or an issue with a medication they are taking. There may be an ongoing sleep issue as opposed to a circumstantial issue such as lack of sleep the previous night, a specific stressor (for example, a lot of schoolwork to complete), or a relationship issue. If Grumpmeister is a persistent problem, addressing potential underlying reasons will become important.

Examples of Grumpmeister

- Akeen frowns at being wakened in the morning. He pulls the covers over his head and makes a snarky comment when asked to get up and prepare for school. His parents know that it is one of those mornings and that they will have to deal with his negative and grumpy mood.

- Akeen gets off the bus and walks into school. He doesn't really look at anyone or talk to anyone. Even when one of his classmates gives a friendly greeting and says, "Hey Akeen", he only grunts a response.

- As the day begins, Akeen must pull out his math book and begin to engage with academic material. He begrudgingly does so with a very sour look on his face and, when asked a question by his teacher, quickly says "I don't know" in a sarcastic tone.

Tips for When Grumpmeister Shows Up

- Consider the circumstances of the situation as well as what underlying causes may be affecting the person's particular mood (for example, lack of sleep, hunger, hurt feelings about something). Calmly ask if any of these suspicions may be true. For example, "You seem tired to me today. Are you feeling tired?" (See: Feelings Investigator and Healthy Tools—Heart)

- Express a desire to help the person through the situation. Remind them of your role ("Hey, I'm your friend," "I'm just trying to help you," or "I am looking out for you") and show a desire to work with them respectfully. (See: Captain Courageous)

- Suggest a time-out or time away if the irritability becomes too intense. State that the issue can be discussed when both parties feel calmer or are in a better place to address the issue. (See: Helpful Coach)

One-Way Street

One-Way Street only sees things one way: their way. This Disconnector has difficulty moving away from their perspective. When other points of view are shared with One-Way Street, they typically respond with their own opinion, insight, or belief. This in turn does not allow for effective communication or understanding. It also diminishes the chance to problem-solve or collaborate.

Due to their inflexibility, One-Way Street misses details and pieces of information that would allow them to adopt a different or broader perspective. This Disconnector is often unaware that another person might think another way about a situation. They may also lack an understanding of how another person could possibly ever think differently. One-Way Street typically lacks skills to recognize this in another person.

One-Way Street also shows up when one has decided that there is nothing redeemable, possible, or intelligent about another person's point of view. One-Way Street paves the road for arguments, frustration, and lack of tolerance as they do not give much respect to the other person's point of view. One-Way Street can appear stubborn or lacking in perspective. Experiencing One-Way Street can be quite annoying for the other person.

Common Behaviors of One-Way Street

Behavior 1: Inflexible Responses

One-Way Street often responds with repetitive and insistent reasoning. They show little ability or willingness to acknowledge another's position or their thoughts.

Behavior 2: Repetition

One-Way Street tends to sound repetitious. They either repeat themselves or reiterate their position with different words, but essentially stating the same thing. Therefore the conversation feels like it goes nowhere if not in alignment with One-Way Street's thinking.

Behavior 3: Apparent Stubbornness

One-Way Street is ready to argue. They do not concede a point, veer from their perspective, or acknowledge that there may be another way to view a situation. They hold tight to their way of thinking and insist the other person is wrong.

Common Responses to One-Way Street

Response 1: Arguing

When trying to feel heard or understood by One-Way Street, a person may engage in an argument, often with much effort to attempt connection and understanding. In arguing, a person may try to show One-Way Street why they need to expand their thinking and reasoning.

Response 2: Exasperation

When One-Way Street does not move from their position or way of thinking, they can leave a person feeling exasperated and exhausted. One-Way Street's insistent reasoning and lack of understanding may also cause disbelief.

Response 3: Avoidance

When One-Way Street is unwilling or unable to listen and acknowledge the other person's thoughts or ideas, shutting down or ending the conversation can seem like the only response left. With nothing left to say and no connection occurring through understanding, a person may walk away and leave the interaction.

Examples of One-Way Street

- George continues to argue with his younger brother insisting that he is right and his brother is wrong. He is not willing to even entertain what his brother is saying.

- Larry and Amanda are in high school and have been dating for a year. Amanda is upset with Larry and vice versa. They are arguing over a comment he made to her, which upset her and she interpreted as a put-down. He cannot understand how she could take it that way and she cannot understand how he could have meant it differently.

- Raj is playing at the Lego bin during indoor recess. His friend is also playing and building a city out of Legos. Raj claims that is not how those Lego pieces are meant to be used and insists they are obviously spaceship Legos which must be used to build spaceships.

Tips for When One-Way Street Shows Up

- Introduce another perspective in a non-threatening way. "Would you be willing to consider a different thought about this?" or "I don't think about this in the same way that you do. Can I tell you what I think?" (See: Two-Way Street and Healthy Tools—Connecting Voice)

- Align with and understand their feelings. This would sound something like, "Let me make sure that I understand. You feel ____ because ____." This can encourage them to let their defenses down and increase their tolerance or openness when discussing other ways to perceive the situation at hand. (See: Feelings Investigator and Healthy Tools—Heart)

- Use visual strategies such as a Venn Diagram that shows how two different thoughts or viewpoints share similarities and differences. This highlights and concretely shows different ways of thinking and the connections between them. This tactic shares a different perspective in a non-threatening manner. (See: Two-Way Street and Healthy Tools—Thinking Brain)

DEFENSES

The Defenses are specific actions used by the Disconnectors. Defenses are behaviors that individuals use to avoid responsibility, cover up where they lack insight, or fight back in a given situation.

Defense 1: I'm Stronger

In this defense, a person shows up acting as if or possibly believing that they are stronger and are going to win. It may be an argument, disagreement, or lobbying against something that they do not want to do or do not agree with in that moment. This defense maintains their current position and intensifies the negative interaction by using power.

Defense 2: Verbal Barrage

This can be a defense or attack. When an individual uses the verbal barrage, they may argue without listening, talk at length without considering another perspective, or continue to talk or yell from their emotional point of view.

Defense 3: Bullhorn

The Bullhorn occurs when a person is loud and overbearing with their words and communication. They may try to forcefully argue their point or become very upset, depending on the situation. They communicate from an emotional or forceful point of view.

Defense 4: Hard Hit

It is painful to be on the receiving end of the Hard Hit. This Defense may be verbal, physical, or behavioral. Fueled by negative emotion, the Hard Hit lashes out. It often comes out of anger but may sometimes be due to unfair treatment. Either way, the consequence is typically hurtful to whomever receives it.

Defense 5: Lightning Strike

The Lightning Strike is a quick response which may be impulsive or meant to destabilize. It comes fast and the other person does not expect the reaction or behavior to come that quickly. It stings when on the receiving end.

CHAPTER 6

Building and Strengthening Connector Skills

Putting these characters into practical use allows adults, children, and teens to recognize how they "show up" in any given situation. Often we do not recognize if we are showing up in a way that further perpetuates the conflict, and if we do, we may not see how to shift to a more productive interaction. Naming and recognizing these characters for oneself as well as communicating with others when there is conflict is an important use of these characters and the main reason they were created. The Connectors are also meant to illustrate specific skill sets which can be modeled or acknowledged in lieu of Disconnector traits.

A general introduction and explanation of the characters to children and teens is recommended prior to using them in a moment of tension. However, adults can adopt and model the skill sets even if their child or teen has not yet been exposed to them. Education and training for each character and skill set, and their use is available at www.tishtaylor.com.

How to Introduce and Apply the Characters

Level 1:

First, learn and understand the system and characters. The best way to model, coach, or reinforce their use is to understand what the characters represent and how to recognize them in everyday situations. Once you understand the concepts and skills, practicing the skill sets will prepare you to teach the Connector system.

Level 2:

Review the characters, including who they are and what they generally represent, with your child or teen. This should include examples that illustrate how the characters show up within realistic scenarios that resonate with their life experiences. Depending on the child's age and, all of the characters may be introduced at one time or instead a few characters at a time to minimize overwhelm. Choosing a few specific, relevant characters may be reasonable and all that is needed in some cases. The characters can be used as an entire set or in combinations that focus on the most important skills for a particular child.

Level 3:

As characters show up in situations, refer to them by name. For example:

> "This sounds like One-Way Street."
>
> "I wonder what Two-Way Street would think?"
>
> "What would Helpful Coach do?"

Making quick references to the characters and their concepts will prompt self-awareness and elicit more appropriate or expected responses in the situation. The same effect can also occur by using the visual card to reference the concepts, without saying much of anything. For example, you may point to the picture or state, "I think I hear [Disconnector]" and hold up the picture. In some instances or with certain children, this may be less confrontational.

Level 4:

Use the phrase "Who is showing up in this moment?" This will prompt the child to think about one or more than one character and analyze how they appear. If they do not respond or seem to know, this can be prompted, such as "It sounds like Deflector". This approach is helping to make the child more self-aware and use the various character concepts.

Level 5:

Reference specific characters and skill sets. This level addresses working on identified and wanted skills in the moment. The child should have already been exposed to and understand the skill sets. This level generalizes the skills in different contexts and situations. For example:

> "Captain Courageous would recognize how he cares about our family and think about what to do even when mad."

> "Shoes would consider their sister's feelings in this situation. How do you think she feels?"

> "Mending in Action would find a way to apologize or make the situation right for both of you.

How can you do that?"

If the child does not give a response, further clarification or modeling can be used such as:

> "Captain Courageous would say, 'I don't want to argue'."

> "Shoes would understand and think about how their sister is feeling disappointed by the mean comment."

> "Mending in Action would offer to share their Halloween candy as a way to repair the big argument over stealing Halloween candy."

Illustrative Examples

This section provides case examples and tips that demonstrate how to put the Who Is Showing Up? concepts into action. In any of the specific scenarios, one may choose to highlight how one or more of the Disconnectors is showing up or just choose to illustrate and model the more appropriate Connector characters. The overarching goal, however, is to recognize, model, coach, or reinforce the most adaptive skills.

Note that the Disconnector characters are not meant to be used in an accusatory manner, but rather informational. For example, in the midst of a tense interaction, "You are such a Deflector!" would be ineffective. Instead, "It seems like we all have a role in what is happening right now" would illustrate the Connector skill set in a manner that is more easily accepted and digested, especially if emotions are heightened.

Example 1: Kate lost screen time.

Kate is very upset because she has lost her phone and screen-time privileges. Beside herself, she slammed her bedroom door and is now in her room furious and sulking. Since Kate is not allowed to communicate with her friends, how is she supposed to know what is going on? What else is she supposed to do if she can't talk to them? She yells at her mother that she has "nothing else to do and will miss out on everything." Her mother has removed this privilege due to Kate's disrespectful behavior and lack of follow-through with her personal responsibilities such as schoolwork and chores. Kate has been more focused on her friends and virtual life than on tending to her family and responsibilities.

Build Connector Skills:

1. When the situation is calmer and Kate acknowledges that she is ready to discuss the situation, her mother can refer to a variety of Disconnector characters to assist Kate with self-awareness and consideration of how she wants to show up. These Disconnectors can include the **Deflector** (not accepting responsibility for herself, then blaming her mother for taking away her devices), **One-Way Street** (seeing the situation from her point of view and not considering others' points of view that she is ignoring family and school

responsibilities), and the **Fighter** (arguing about the consequence, and making continual references to why it is wrong and why her mother is unfair).

2. Conversely, making use of the Connectors can be helpful in this situation. For example, **Two-Way Street** understands that avoiding or putting off one's responsibilities impacts others. This includes Kate's family scrambling to help her with assignments at the last minute because she is totally stressed. Kate not completing her share of chores around the house ends up placing the responsibility on others to complete them. Two-Way Street could help correct both of these examples in which Kate's behavior creates stress for her family and requires action from others.

3. **Shoes** would help Kate to imagine how it feels to be yelled at, ignored, and disrespected. Asking her to consider how it feels to be on the receiving end of her behavior may help her better understand her mother's reaction.

4. Lastly, **Captain Courageous** (hopefully Kate, but if not, her mother) would return to the situation with a problem-solving mindset, approach it respectfully, and try to work out a plan and solution together. After all, enforcing consequences is not fun for parents either.

Example 2: Sam struggles in the classroom.

Sam doesn't understand why his teacher is frustrated with him. She tells Sam that "he is not putting forth his best effort in this class." Sam struggles with sustained focus in class, often thinks that he already knows the information (to some extent he does), and frequently pulls out an unrelated book or other materials during class. He does so when his teacher expects him to be paying attention to the lesson, and he doesn't realize that his teacher interprets this behavior as disrespectful and resistant.

Build Connector Skills:

1. The teacher could take time after class to communicate to Sam that he is showing up as the Disconnector **No Way**. Explaining to him that he seems not to follow instructions like his classmates and appears to determine his own rules provides an opportunity for Sam to express what he is thinking and feeling. Maybe he is bored and thinks he knows the information, or maybe he feels overwhelmed. Either way, this type of communication will allow Sam a chance to understand and express his **Feelings Mind**.

2. On another level, Sam is also acting as an **Insulator**, escaping through reading which allows him to disconnect and remain less stressed. Sam is not showing insight into how he appears to others and why the teacher would react to him the way that she does. Utilizing **Feelings Investigator** can help Sam understand the message that his behavior sends to fellow classmates. They see him not following directions and that leads to a more challenging situation for the teacher as she tries to maintain fairness and cooperation in the classroom. Considering the teacher's situation and the way his behavior impacts her efforts to manage classroom behaviors so that everyone can learn will provide Sam with additional insight.

3. Sam or his teacher can show up as **Captain Courageous** by using insight from both of their perspectives, building greater understanding between them, and then implementing specific ideas for how to move forward given what they understand.

Example 3: David blows up.

David had a heated argument with his parents because they would not allow him to drive his friends to a party. He became very mad because he had already promised his friends that he would pick them up and made specific plans with them. His parents stated that this was his first time driving at night and they were not okay with him taking friends as well. The situation ended with David being grounded for the evening for shouting at his parents, calling them "horrible parents," "jerks," and "idiots," slamming doors, and screaming at them for not understanding anything.

Build Connector Skills:

1. When all are calm, the situation can be addressed by first assessing how David was showing up. To his parents, David showed up as the Disconnectors **Fighter** and **Deflector** by resorting to a heated and disrespectful argument when things did not go his way and he felt his parents seemed unfair. He also deflected responsibility for promising a ride to his friends without permission, especially since it would have been a first-time privilege.

2. It may be fair to consider if David's parents were showing up as **One-Way Street** by not listening to his concern or helping problem-solve the situation. **Two-Way Street** may have been possible if all parties were able to remain calm and consider both points of view. Two-Way Street would recognize the parents' perspective around safety as well as David's perspective about having to break a promise to his friends

3. **Mending in Action** is important in this type of conflict, since this Connector shows up by acknowledging each role and wanting to make the situation better. Mending in Action includes communicating care and consideration for each other, even if both David and his parents are upset about what occurred. Using **Healthy Tools** (**Connecting Voice and Eyes**) will assist Mending in Action with a calm voice and eye contact to engage in connection and maintain attention to the other person.

4. Other helpful Connectors in this situation may include **Feelings Investigator** with could assist David with understanding how other parents may feel about a first-time driver chauffeuring their teenager at night to a party and how they may not have known about these

plans. Lastly, **Helpful Coach** can recognize that prior to the situation blowing up, taking a time-out to try and be as rational as possible would have been more productive.

Example 4: Bella melts down at the store.

Bella is at the department store with her parents and sees a vintage lamp that she really wants for her room. Her parents are willing to help her update her room and have talked about purchasing some new items. However, this particular lamp is quite expensive and many cheaper options are available. Bella insists that this is the lamp she wants. She argues that she has kept up with her chores and schoolwork after all. Bella accuses her parents of caring more about her brother than about her as they bought him an expensive item for his room. Her parents feel that she is quite demanding, not considerate or caring about what she asks, and not fully cognizant of the situation and money spent for her brother. They determine not to buy the lamp and leave the store with Bella furious at them.

Build Connector Skills:

1. When everyone is calmer, the concept of **One-Way Street** can be referenced as well as the **Fighter**, since Bella only thought about this from her perspective and provided various aggressive arguments as to why she should be able to have the item without considering another point of view.

2. In encouraging Bella to consider her approach when she wants something, suggestions can include putting herself in the **Shoes** of the person she is asking. Her parents can explain that it is important to consider how another person feels when she asks them to do something without gratitude or consideration for their situation. In addition, requesting something via demand and insistence elicits a much more negative response and distaste for the situation on the receiving end.

3. Bella's parents can suggest, model, and coach how **Healthy Tools** like **Active Listening** and an **Open Heart** are important in order to better understand one other. Listening to what her parents have to say about expensive purchases and what is different about this situation compared to the situation with her brother would allow Bella another perspective—another instance of **Two-Way Street**. Ultimately connection and understanding are more important than any item from a store.

Example 5: Kelly is fed up.

Kelly is so tired of his mother telling him to stop focusing on video games and YouTube and to do something else. He feels like she is always on his case and his frustration level is very high at this point. Doesn't she see what he does do? What is the problem with having downtime anyway? He spends all day at school and will get everything done on his own time. She nags too much, according to him. So on this particular day, when his mother again states that he needs to do something else or get his chores and homework done, Kelly feels very frustrated and tells her to "leave me alone," "stop nagging me," and that "none of my friends' mothers are this annoying."

Build Connector Skills:

1. In this instance, Kelly's mother faces a choice in how she responds. With the assistance of **Feelings Mind**, she can label her feelings as very frustrated, probably angry. She is at her wit's end over Kelly's lack of response and of attention to anything but screens until he is told to stop multiple times or given the threat of a consequence. Her natural reaction is to yell at Kelly and essentially lecture him about this entire situation and how it feels for her. However, she also has the choice to deliver her message in a dignified manner, which may include potential consequences but can be stated in a way that maintains a Connecting delivery. Her approach may rely on **Two-Way Street** and **Shoes**, acknowledging how Kelly would like downtime, how he looks forward to it, and how she can understand that.

2. While understanding and considering the above, it is also important for Kelly to show up as a **Feelings Investigator** and recognize how his choices and behavior impact others. When he chooses to put off responsibilities and prolong his downtime, this choice impacts his family's nighttime routine and how late others may have to stay up. In addition, when he does not finish his chores in a timely manner, this affects others: for example, not unloading the dishwasher and cleaning the sink now makes these chores his mother's responsibility as she has to make dinner.

Example 6: Stephan is grouchy.

Simone asks herself, "How many mornings can this go on? I can hardly take it anymore!" She does the best that she can to allow for a peaceful morning and jump through hoops to help Stephan wake up on time and in a reasonable mood. However, waking Stephan up in the morning is often like poking a bear and she just holds her breath each day. Stephan is often difficult and will blame Simone for the day starting.

Build Connector Skills:

1. Showing up as **Feelings Mind** with a calm reflection can be helpful. For example, "I am trying to help you," or "I am willing to help you, but we both need to be respectful to each other." **Shoes** also helps to verbalize the child's feelings such as, "I know you are tired and that you want a little more sleep, I understand."

2. Using **Healthy Tools** such as **Breath** and **Connecting Voice** can be helpful in that they remind a person to breathe through the moment, not let frustration take over, and keep one's voice calm. These connecting tools can provide an example of how to start the day more peacefully. These skills help counteract Stephan showing up as **Grumpmeister**.

3. Using **Healthy Tools—Thinking Brain** can allow for problem-solving the night before. For example, Simone and Stephan

can brainstorm how to start the day when it is time to wake up so that it will be peaceful for all. Prior to going to sleep, alternative approaches to the order of the morning routine or the mindset needed for morning may be shared more openly. Whatever it may be, allowing for problem-solving prior to the situation can be helpful.

Example 7: Sally argues with her father.

Sally and her father disagree about specific political and social issues. Sally is typically quite opinionated and self-assured about a variety of topics. In this particular instance, she and her father each feel quite passionate about their particular position on climate change and what they each see as "right." Their argument turns counterproductive and begins to annoy the rest of the family who are tired of hearing the two of them argue and debate.

Build Connector Skills:

1. Vehement arguing does not typically change the other person's mind. Utilizing the **Helpful Coach** could help clear the air. Sally or her father could suggest taking a break from the issue or the argument as it only serves to make each person angrier or more upset. This would help avoid either or both of them storming off, turning into the **Insulator**, and not talking to each other.

2. Showing up with a **Feelings Mind** helps with recognizing one's goal in this moment. What do you want to accomplish and what is getting accomplished? If it is only arguing and frustration, then disconnection is the likely outcome.

3. Sally and her father could introduce **Two-Way Street** or language that sounds like it. Is there a way to consider another perspective? Would Sally or her father be open to at least hearing or considering the other's perspective, even if not agreeing? If both accept that respect for each other is an important value, then this instance requires it.

4. It also takes a caring **Heart** (**Healthy Tools**) to consider what someone you love may think or feel, even if it opposes your position and belief system. One may never change another's viewpoint or feelings on an issue, but the disagreement can be approached with dignity toward the other person.

Additional Tips

Establish and Convey Your Values

Don't forget to remind yourself and your child *why* you advocate, suggest, or request a certain behavior. The situation can consistently return to a place of connection and understanding if we establish the important values that we strive to meet. For example, we value respect, dignity, and consideration in our family and our behavior should match those values.

Timing

The Who Is Showing Up? system is created to address behavioral patterns that occur with varying degrees of frequency. But when Disconnector behavior patterns are frequent, conflict, frustration, and relationship strain will increase. Knowing when to bring up a character or behavior pattern is an important technique. Should you do it in the moment? Or later, when all persons involved are calmer? Should you involve a third party if a simple discussion risks instigating another conflict? It depends. Consider all of your options in regard to timing, and proceed with the best course of action. Most individuals are not open to constructive feedback when very angered or oppositional. It is important to teach these characters when the situation is open for learning. That may mean abstaining from tackling the issue when you or your child are upset, unless they are motivated to show up in another way and are open to the feedback.

Show Caring Reflection, Not Name-Calling

I have found that showing non-threatening reflection and presenting Disconnector and Connector characters in a manner that is caring, respectful, and honest have the greatest chance to resonate in the moment or even after the situation has occurred. Remember that all of us are vulnerable and tend to defend ourselves when something negative is being pointed out to us. Some can turn the negativity on themselves internally. Therefore, it is important not to present these characters and their description in a moment of anger or frustration, since that risks conveying a negative comment on their person. If the situation is heightened in an angry way, the message will likely not be communicated in the manner intended and instead will be interpreted as a put-down or criticism. In most instances, your introduction of the characters will not be heard and may be something else for your child to defend themselves against. It is very important that the characters not be presented in a shaming manner, such as "look at how you are showing up again!", but instead in a manner meant for guidance and self-reflection.

Be Creative

Using creativity when bringing these characters into needed moments of conflict or difficulty is also appropriate. Each family or person may think of an instructive or meaningful approach that works for them. For example, using a different accent to deliver the message is a fun and creative approach and allows for some humor when targeting problematic behaviors.

Focus On the Positive

Don't forget to notice when your child or teen is showing signs and behaviors that are connecting. They may not do it consistently or wholly, but when they do in certain moments or situations, notice the attempt. Building on the positive is typically an easier path to behavior improvement.

It May Not Happen Overnight

I have found that many children understand the concepts of the Disconnectors and Connectors. They may even understand how they show up in specific examples, but they cannot necessarily generalize the concepts to all situations and examples, nor can they easily apply these new concepts and change a behavior pattern. As with many other concepts that work to change thinking and behavior patterns, generalization and implementation can take time and require ongoing coaching. They also work most effectively if the Connector behaviors are being modeled for them.

What If the Disconnectors Persist?

What does one do if the Disconnector behaviors persist and are resistant to change? At this point, professional help may likely be warranted if not already sought. Consider analyzing the situation from different angles that could explain why there is resistance. Is there something internal about the child's mood, affect, or personality that makes change more difficult? Is there something about the behavior that provides a reinforcement for them in some way? What is the level of motivation to change or the belief that they can change? If either or both of these are low, that would be an issue to address therapeutically. In addition, utilization of different treatment types or modalities should be considered if they have not already been tried. Another point of consideration would be the lack of insight about themselves: self-reflection and perceiving how one "shows up" can be more difficult for some individuals. Further direct teaching may likely be warranted, which typically would involve professional assistance.

In Conclusion

The ultimate goal of the Who Is Showing Up? system is to create more connection and decrease unnecessary conflict within families and between adults, children, and teens. Having communication tools at your disposal, such as the Connectors and Disconnectors, will hopefully help you understand, communicate, and follow through with what is valued and most important in your life: your relationships. Practicing and modeling the Connector skill sets into everyday behavior is not always an easy task, particularly in the face of frustration. But the skill sets are achievable and provide a roadmap for improvement. We all walk a journey in each of our relationships as well as in the greater dynamic within our families. This system is designed to help your relationships flourish over time, even in the face of significant challenges. My hope is for you to remain connected with your child or teen into their adulthood and, when you can look back, to know that you did your best to maintain a respectful and loving relationship.

REFERENCES

Actmindfully.com.au/alookatyourvalues

Booker, J.A., Ollendick, T.H., Dunsmore, J.C., & Greene, R.W. (2016). *Perceived parent-child relations, conduct problems, and clinical improvement following the treatment of oppositional defiant disorder.* Journal of Child and Family Studies, 25, 1623–1633.

Claire, K. & Werner-Wilson, R. (2013). *From John Lee to John Gottman: Recognizing intra- and interpersonal differences to promote marital satisfaction.* Journal of Human Sciences 1(2): 32–46.

Diagnostic and Statistical Manual of Mental Health Disorders (2013). American Psychiatric Publishing.

Doherty, M. (2009). *Theory of mind: How children understand others' thoughts and feelings.* Psychology Press.

Gottman, John M. (1999). *The seven principles for making marriage work.* Three Rivers Press.

Harris, Russ (2010). *A Quick Look at your Values.* https://www.actmindfully.com.au/wp-content/uploads/2019/07/Values_Checklist_-_Russ_Harris.pdf

Miller-Slough, R.L., Dunsmore, J.C., Ollendick, T.H., & Greene, R.W. (2016). *Parent–child synchrony in children with oppositional defiant disorder: Associations with treatment outcomes.* Journal of Child and Family Studies, 25, 1880–1888.

ABOUT THE AUTHOR

Dr. Tish Taylor

Dr. Tish Taylor is a licensed psychologist with a private practice in the greater Kansas City area. She has an established practice helping children, teens, and their families. She is also a licensed school psychologist and has years of experience working within school districts as a psychologist and coordinator of mental health services. In addition, Dr. Taylor is an adjunct professor teaching Child Development for many years. She has previously written a book entitled *Parenting ADHD with Wisdom and Grace*.

www.ingramcontent.com/pod-product-compliance
Lightning Source LLC
Chambersburg PA
CBHW042146290426
44110CB00003B/134